SAVORY
DINNER PIES

Inspiring | Educating | Creating | Entertaining

Brimming with creative inspiration, how-to projects, and useful information to enrich your everyday life, quarto.com is a favorite destination for those pursuing their interests and passions.

© 2021 Quarto Publishing Group USA Inc.
Text © 2021 Ken Haedrich
Photography © 2021 Melissa DiPalma

First Published in 2021 by The Harvard Common Press, an imprint of The Quarto Group, 100 Cummings Center, Suite 265-D, Beverly, MA 01915, USA.
T (978) 282-9590 F (978) 283-2742 Quarto.com

The Harvard Common Press titles are also available at discount for retail, wholesale, promotional, and bulk purchase. For details, contact the Special Sales Manager by email at specialsales@quarto.com or by mail at The Quarto Group, Attn: Special Sales Manager, 100 Cummings Center, Suite 265-D, Beverly, MA 01915, USA.

25 24 23 22   2 3 4 5

ISBN: 978-0-7603-7359-0

Digital edition published in 2021
eISBN: 978-0-7603-7360-6

Library of Congress Cataloging-in-Publication Data

Haedrich, Ken, 1954-
Dinner pies : from shepherd's pies and pot pies to tarts, turnovers, quiches, hand pies, and more, with 100 delectable and foolproof recipes / Ken Haedrich.
pages cm
Includes index.
ISBN 978-1-55832-851-8 (hardback)
1. Potpies. 2. Casserole cooking. 3. Stews. I. Title.
TX693.H25 2015
641.82'1--dc23
2015018097

Design: Ashley Prine, Tandem Books
Cover Images: Melissa DiPalma
Spine and Back Cover Texture: Global Zen/shutterstock
Page Layout: Ashley Prine, Tandem-Books

Printed in USA

SAVORY DINNER PIES

More Than 80 Delicious Recipes from Around the World

Ken Haedrich

HARVARD COMMON PRESS

CONTENTS

AUTHOR'S NOTE

Hello, my name is Ken and I am hopelessly addicted to crust. I've been this way for decades. In fact, I can scarcely remember eating a meal that I felt could not have been improved by putting some sort of crust over, under, or around it. Serve me a thick soup or a hearty stew, and all I can think is how much better it would have been as a pot pie. A platter of plain vegetables leaves me reimagining them in an open-faced galette, enriched with a bit of cream and cheese. That braised kale and sausage? Shame they weren't cozied up together in a hand pie with some provolone cheese, and a dish of tomato sauce on the side. (And I wonder why I never get invited over for dinner.)

Don't even get me started on crustless quiche, a notion I find just plain disturbing.

I am, in short, what you could call a dinner pie fanatic. It doesn't matter to me if it's filled with a savory custard, like a quiche, or if it's handheld, big, small, saucy, meatless, or chock-full o' beef. We're just one big, happy, extended crusted family in my book—literally—and we all get along beautifully.

If any of this resonates—if you, too, have a lust for crust—you have found a comrade in the kitchen. I welcome you with open arms. In the pages that follow I promise to indulge your passion for dinner pies with unmitigated zeal.

Even if you don't share my extreme appetite for a dinner pie universe, however, I sincerely hope you will join me on this exploration of crusted cuisine. How could you not? Indeed, how could anyone ignore a category so ripe with potential, so picturesque—could there be a dish more fetching than a free-form tomato tart baked to golden perfection at the peak of summer?—so versatile, and so perfectly suited for special occasions.

Wouldn't you prefer to flatter your guests with, say, a Caramelized Onion, Bacon, and Swiss Cheese Pie (page 132), homemade crust flaking into a thousand buttery shards, than issue forth something mundane in an anonymous frozen pie shell? It's a no-brainer, isn't it? This is cuisine that lets you strut your stuff in the kitchen, capture the essence of the season in a crust, and score bigtime with family and guests.

Being something of a mind reader in matters of pastry and crust, I know what you might be thinking (if, that is, you're not already sprinting toward the car, shopping list in hand). You're thinking you couldn't make a homemade pie pastry even if your life depended on it. You've tried. You've bungled. You've failed. You've more or less given up. You weren't born with the pie dough gene. And you haven't gotten over the dreadful memory of your dough flying apart in midair while your boyfriend (spouse, mother, brother) laughed like a hyena, scarring you for life. (I agree: He or she is a jerk.)

Well, I've heard it all before, in spades, and I can help. I know this because when I'm not writing cookbooks, I'm the "dean" of ThePieAcademy.com, where I teach folks just like you how to make great pies, both sweet and savory. These folks arrive at my virtual doorstep, unload their pie pastry baggage, and let me know, in no uncertain terms, that they are hopeless.

They are not. And neither are you.

Which is to say I've done my best to anticipate the questions you're likely to have about making pie doughs and dinner pies, and I have filled these pages with useful advice, tips, and techniques that will help you overcome your fear of pie making. I've included discussions about my favorite dinner pie tools and equipment, the best methods for rolling your dough and getting it into the pan, and instructions for how to prebake your pie shell when you're making a quiche. All this, plus my thoughts on pantry ingredients, and a guide to shopping for produce, too.

And now, it's up to you. You're holding the manual, the ingredients you need are within easy reach, and now you simply have to find something that looks good and get busy. If you're an old hand at dinner pies, I think you'll discover plenty of new ideas to get you excited about your craft. If you're a relative newcomer, I hope you'll embrace your dinner pie "beginner's mind"— that Zen quality of openness, eagerness, and curiosity that comes with new exploration. Proceed with confidence and savor the outcome of your efforts with those you love. And if you do happen to run into any obstacles, just send me an email (ken@thepieacademy.com), and I'll do my best to help you find a solution.

Ken Haedrich
The Coastal Carolinas

INTRODUCTION

What It Takes to Make the Perfect Dinner Pie

In this introduction, I will tell you all about the tools and ingredients that make for perfect dinner pies. At the end of this section, I'll reveal the simple tricks I've learned over the years that make working with doughs and pastries relatively trouble-free—and much easier than you might have thought.

TOOLS OF THE TRADE

Part of the fun of making pies, whether savory or sweet, is collecting the tools that make the process more enjoyable and the outcome more fetching. I recommend that you spend a little more and buy quality stuff that you won't have to replace every couple of years.

Pie Pans

Quite a few of the pies in this book are baked in everyday pie pans (also known as pie plates or pie tins), with sloping sides, and many of the quiche recipes that call for a tart pan can successfully be baked in a pie pan as well. My collection of pie pans numbers more than 50—not because I need that many, but because I'm constantly trying out new ones, with different designs and materials, to stay up to date on any improvements or innovations that might benefit the members of my pie-baking community, ThePieAcademy.com. Plus, I just like pie pans.

If a hurricane were on the way, always a possibility here in coastal North Carolina, and I could grab only four pie pans on my way out the door, I'd choose one metal pan, one clay pan, one Pyrex pan, and one stoneware pan.

If you want a rugged, well-made pie pan that will probably outlast you, buy the 9-inch aluminized steel pie pan made by USA Pan. The

deep-dish clay pan I adore is made by Tom Hess of Hess Pottery in Missouri (hesspottery.com).

No discussion of pie pans would be complete without mentioning the rugged and reasonably priced pie pans made by Pyrex. I find their smaller, shallow pans too skimpy for a pie of any consequence. But their 9½-inch Flavor Savor deep-dish pans with handles—and an even deeper one they call the Easy Grab pan, which has a fluted edge—are great for dinner pies.

In the stoneware realm, Le Creuset and Emile Henry are my favorite pie pan manufacturers. The physical beauty of all three makes them great presentation pans if you're bringing a pie from oven to table.

Individual Pie Pans for Pot Pies and Small Pies

Like my regular pie pans, my individual pie pan collection has gotten a little out of hand. These things follow me home like stray kittens and I can't seem to turn any away.

Many of the smaller pie recipes in this collection will give a range, such as 4 to 6, for the number of servings they yield. This range is because small pie pans come in such a variety of depths and diameters that it's difficult to be absolute. The capacity can run anywhere from ¾ cup to about 1½ cups, and the diameter from 3 inches (for a ramekin) to 6 inches.

The key to a good individual pot pie pan is choosing one that results in a nicely balanced proportion of crust to filling. I think about 5 inches across and 1½ inches deep is just about perfect for a hearty serving. If a pot pie is very rich, or if I want to stretch the recipe to feed more people, I use a smaller pan, say 4 or 4¼ inches across and 1 inch deep. Often I find myself reaching for my individual-size disposable aluminum pans for pies I plan to give away or stash in the freezer.

Tart Pans

Quite a few of the dinner pies in this collection are made in a tart pan, sometimes called a quiche pan. These pans have straight sides, not sloped. I really like the way a quiche looks when it's been baked in a tart pan. It's got drama, fluted sides (which most tart pans have), and an attractive low profile that doesn't tower over everything else on your plate.

If you're new to making quiches or tarts, you might want to start with a single-piece stoneware tart pan; Le Creuset is a good bet in this department.

The main drawback to heavy stoneware pans is that the density of the material can inhibit the browning of the crust, especially the bottom crust, sometimes resulting in a crust that's not "done" as much as it could be. To offset this tendency, I often start my stoneware-baked pies and tarts low in the oven, closer to the bottom heat source, to help brown the crust. Then I move the rack and tart up about midway through the baking.

Metal tart pans come in a range of shapes and sizes, including square and rectangular, but 95 percent of the time I use my 9½-inch-diameter, 1-inch-deep pan. This pan has fluted sides that yield a pretty ruffled edge to the finished tart. The sides are just a little lower than is ideal, so to increase the height of the sides, be sure to fold your overhanging dough over and into the pan, pressing it against the sides, which will extrude it upward, ¼ inch or so above the top of the pan. That doesn't sound like much, but that little bit of extra height can accommodate quite a bit more filling. There's a version of this same pan with 2-inch sides that comes in handy when you want a generously proportioned quiche.

The thing most bakers love about the removable-bottom pans is just that: Once the tart has cooled off a bit, we can place the tart on a wide can and let the sides drop off, revealing the pretty fluted crust.

Anything made in a removable-bottom tart pan should be baked on top of a baking sheet, preferably one lined with parchment paper.

Finally, another bottomless pan that's great for tarts is known as a flan ring or tart ring. You place the ring on a lined baking sheet; the sheet acts as the bottom of the pan. Line this arrangement with your pastry, and you're good to go. The thing I love most about my flan ring is the size: 10 inches in diameter by 1½ inches deep, perfect for a crowd.

Baking Sheets

Like pie pans, the main thing you're looking for in a baking sheet is good weight and durability. A heavy, rugged sheet is less likely to buckle, and that matters if you've just uploaded a custardy quiche into a hot oven: You want that filling to stay put, not catapult onto your oven walls.

My rule of thumb for dinner pies and baking sheets is this: If there's a chance that the filling or anything else will spill onto and then run off the sheet, I use a rimmed one. If there's virtually no chance, I go rimless, mainly because it's easier to get baked things on and off a rimless sheet. Like the pie pan I mentioned, USA Pan baking sheets are my favorites.

Parchment Paper

It's hard to overstate how much easier my life as a pie maker has become since I got turned on to parchment paper. I buy it in large, 16 x 24-inch sheets from an online restaurant-supply store, but you can also buy it in 15-inch-wide rolls at the supermarket. No matter how I use it, parchment saves me time on cleanup. I prepare and roll pastry on it; I accumulate produce scraps and trimmings on it; and I line baking sheets with it. Hell, I'd wrap Christmas presents with it if I thought my wife wouldn't retaliate with a rolling pin upside my head. (See Rolling Pins, below.)

Rolling Pins

Even a prolific pie maker can easily get by with just two rolling pins, possibly even just one. My first choice would be a French-style solid wood (maple or cherry) pin, about 20 inches long, with a slight taper at the ends. The slight taper keeps the dough from wanting to grab onto the pin, and the single-piece-of-wood construction makes it easy to apply firm and direct pressure. We sell just such a pin, made to our specifications, at ThePieAcademy.com online store.

The other pin I couldn't do without is an American-style wood pin, with handles, like the 12-inch classic rolling pin sold by Fletchers' Mill, a Maine company.

I often use both of these pins when I'm rolling out my pie pastry: the tapered one to start the dough, and the larger American-style one with handles to finish it.

Food Processor

I make no bones about the fact that I love my food processor for making pie pastry. Put a food processor and a pastry blender in front of me, and I'll choose the food processor every time. It's quicker than the hand method, and there's simply no basis to the argument that a crust made in the food processor can't match the flavor or flaky-tender texture of a handmade crust.

Your average 9-, 10-, or 11-cup processor will be just fine. For a single crust, a 10- to 12-cup processor is ideal. For a double crust batch of dough, a 14-cup processor is the way to go.

Pastry Blender

A lot of bakers prefer mixing in the traditional manner, cutting the fat into the flour by hand. Some of the more common methods involve doing so literally *by hand*—rubbing vigorously with your fingers—while others suggest using two knives, or

a large pastry fork. But the most popular tool for the job is a pastry blender, which is nothing more than a set of curved wires or blunt blades attached to a handle. The business end is pushed repeatedly into the fat and flour mixture until combined. My favorite is an inexpensive one made by OXO that has wires and a nonslip handle.

Cooling Racks

Several years ago, my wife came home from a Pampered Chef party with a pair of large (10 x 18-inch) cooling racks, with folding legs that keep the racks about 4 inches off the counter. It was love at first sight. Those 4 inches are a big deal, because that means there is plenty of ventilated space underneath, so my pies cool off quicker. And it's enough room that the heat from the pan won't damage a wooden table or countertop the way it could with a squatty cooling rack. These racks are large enough to accommodate any home kitchen baking sheet, and the folding legs make for easy storage.

A GUIDE TO DINNER PIE INGREDIENTS

Virtually everything you need for the recipes in this collection can be found in your average well-stocked supermarket.

Butter

Most bakers agree that unsalted butter—rather than salted—is the way to go. That way, you know you're starting from zero with the salt and you can regulate the precise amount that ends up in your pastry.

I've experimented with many brands of butter of the years, including the big supermarket brand names and the higher-fat European-style butters, and frankly, I've become much less picky about butter than I once was. Some brands might be a little better than others, but I'm happy with the results I get with most supermarket house brands, including Costco unsalted butter, which is my go-to these days. Besides, I use a lot of butter, and I can't really justify paying twice as much for an ingredient when the outcome is only marginally improved, if at all. The best way to decide which butter is right for you is to experiment with different brands.

Vegetable Shortening

While vegetable shortening—what most of us call by its brand name, Crisco—doesn't have butter's buttery flavor or create as flaky a crust, it has plenty of other qualities to recommend it.

It's much more economical than butter, and adding Crisco to your pie crust can make it blessedly easy to handle and roll. It adds considerable tenderness to your crust and helps it hold its shape, too. The majority of dinner pies have plenty of other rich ingredients in them, so using a crust recipe that incorporates a measure of vegetable shortening hardly amounts to a flavor compromise.

My advice: Don't exclude Crisco from your pie crusts, especially if you haven't ever tried it before. Both of my Go-To Pie Dough recipes include it, and if you like those, you can increase the proportion of shortening even more.

Flour

For my day-to-day pie making, I just use one of the big name brands, typically Gold Medal all-purpose flour. All-purpose flours come in bleached and unbleached varieties, and I lean toward the bleached because, as I understand it, the bleaching process "softens" the wheat and you wind up with a more tender crust.

The best whole wheat flour for pie crusts is whole wheat pastry flour. It's milled from soft wheat, which gets you better results than bread flours that are milled from hard wheat.

Eggs and Cheese

Since I use a lot of eggs—in quiches and in my daily cooking—I'm somewhat particular about them and I tend to buy only organic, free-range eggs, because I think that happy chickens lay better-tasting eggs than ones who are caged up.

I divide cheeses into a couple of groupings, starting with the everyday ones you get in the dairy section and are moderately priced. This includes the cheddars, Swiss cheese, Monterey Jack, mozzarella, and several others, in blocks or pre-grated.

And then there's the gourmet cheese section, a panoply of seductively fabulous cheeses from around the world with a gourmet price tag.

As you might guess, I shop in the former section more than the latter. If I have any cheese-buying rule of thumb at all, it's tied to what I think of as the final flavor payoff: If the cheese is competing with a lot of other flavors in a dinner pie, I'll probably use a good everyday cheese. If it's one of the starring flavors, I'll go with a better cheese.

Produce

When I can, I buy locally grown produce, and whenever possible I try to plan my baking around what's in season.

That said, there are some produce staples I try to keep on hand at all times because they form the foundation of flavor and substance for the dinner pie maker.

These staples include the aromatic vegetables—sweet onions, celery, and carrots. You should have garlic on hand, of course, and

HANDS ON: PIE DOUGH PARTICULARS

As the "dean" of ThePieAcademy.com, an online community of passionate pie makers, I'm well aware that there are several key steps in the pie-making process that trip people up: rolling the dough, getting it in the pan, and—as we do with most of our quiches—prebaking the shell. So don't feel bad if your best pie-making intentions have hit a roadblock at one of these junctures. The first thing I'm going to do is try to talk you through these rough patches. And the second thing I'm going to do is encourage you to visit ThePieAcademy.com, where you can find videos to help you with all this stuff. The mixing steps are pretty well covered in the basic dough recipes on pages 22 to 29, so we'll start with rolling, a very common trouble spot.

Rolling Out Your Pie Dough

If you haven't already, you'll soon discover that the majority of recipes in this collection follow a predictable pattern: You make a dough, then refrigerate it for at least 1½ to 2 hours before rolling it out. Longer is fine. We don't refrigerate the dough just so we have time to do the dishes, go grocery shopping, or prep the rest of the ingredients in our dinner pie—though I'll often do one or more of those things during this rest period. We refrigerate the dough so it has time to relax and become uniformly cool, both of which make it easier to roll and, ultimately, more tender and flaky.

After a couple of hours, your dough should be chilled through and through. Because the coolness re-firms the fat, the dough can become rather solid. The higher the proportion of

green bell peppers if you make a lot of Italian dishes. Potatoes are a mainstay of pot pies and shepherd's pie. And I'm seldom without a pound of mushrooms in the fridge, or a big bunch of fresh kale, Swiss chard, collards, or spinach, each of them a great quiche enhancer. I try to go easy on fresh tomatoes unless they're in season, because off-season tomatoes, as you know, are pretty abysmal.

Fresh herbs are the grace notes of cooking, and without them all of our dishes would be lacking. My cabinets are well stocked with dried herbs, too, because, much as I prefer fresh herbs, they aren't always available.

While close to 85 percent of the veggies I cook with are fresh, I'm not one to skip the frozen food aisle. Frozen veggies will never taste like just-picked ones, but the quality can still be pretty decent. Especially in saucy pot pies, frozen vegetables work like a charm.

butter to vegetable shortening in your dough, the more solid it will be. All-butter doughs can be quite firm.

It's a good idea to let a firmed-up dough sit at room temperature for 5 to 10 minutes before you start trying to roll it. Butter is most stable within a fairly narrow temperature range, so once you start rolling, your intention should be to get it rolled and in the pan without delay. This doesn't mean you have to rush. But it does mean you shouldn't pick up the phone and call your BFF once you're under way.

Assuming that you're using moderate pressure on your rolling pin, you shouldn't have to fight the dough. Rather, it should just yield under your pin—not too solid, but not a pushover, either. If the dough is too soft, it's likely to start sticking to both your pin and your work surface before you're done rolling. Not a good thing. (If this happens, just slide it back onto a baking sheet and re-refrigerate it for 10 to 15 minutes.)

When you roll, lightly dust your rolling pin, your work surface, and the top of your dough with flour. You can do this dusting by hand, but I like my little flour shaker, which has a domed screen lid. Use a light touch and don't apply too much flour, lest your guests end up with a mouthful of flour dust, an altogether unpleasant experience that seldom makes a great impression.

What's the best surface to roll on? There are many options and opinions. Everyone seems to have a pet method that they swear by. Some bakers like to place their dough between sheets of plastic wrap and roll it out that way. This works well, but the plastic tends to crimp and require constant fiddling with. Others roll directly on their countertop, be it wood, granite, laminate, or another surface. Still others prefer marble slabs,

because marble is a cool, rolling-friendly surface. But marble is heavy, and unless you can leave it in place, it's a pain to move around.

My favorite methods, one of which I discussed earlier in this chapter, are rolling onto parchment paper and rolling onto wax paper.

In the former, I put a large sheet of parchment paper on a large silicone mat that sits on my granite countertop. I dust the parchment lightly with flour, place my dough in the middle, then dust the dough and begin to roll. After each swipe or two of my rolling pin, I give the dough a little clockwise turn to make sure it isn't sticking. If it is—and if the dough hasn't gotten too big and unwieldy yet—I'll flour the top of the dough, flip it over, and continue to roll until it's as large as I need it. All the while, I'm dusting with flour as necessary, always using a light hand.

When I roll onto wax paper, I do things a little differently. First, I lay the wax paper directly on my smaller (11½ x 16½-inch) silicone mat instead of my large mat. The small mat gives me the maneuverability I'm going to need momentarily. Then I dust the wax paper lightly with flour and begin to roll. In the early stages of rolling, I'll be able to give the dough little clockwise turns. But when the dough starts to grip the paper—it typically will—I rotate the silicone mat itself rather than try to lift the dough off the paper. Once the dough has been rolled, I lift the wax paper off the mat, invert the dough and paper over the pan, center it, then gently peel off the paper. This "releasability" of wax paper is the reason I like it so much for rolling dough. (Keep in mind that wax paper can't be used to line a baking sheet that's going into the oven; always use parchment paper for that.)

One common mistake home bakers make is not easing up on the pressure as they approach the edge of the pastry with the pin. This typically results in the pastry edge flattening out and getting sealed tight to the rolling surface. So, remember to ease off on the pressure as your pin gets close to the edge. Make your pin sort of fly off the edge, parallel to your work surface, so you don't pinch the dough.

You can buy rolling pins with silicone rings on the ends that enable you to roll the dough to a predetermined thickness; I think of them as training wheels. Despite their popularity, I'm not a big fan because, like training wheels, they give the user a false sense of control. Better that you should just roll your dough a little unevenly at first, while you're in training. That's the best way to develop the right touch and attain actual pie dough mastery in the process.

Getting the Dough into Your Pan

You have all sorts of options for getting your pie pastry off your rolling surface and into your pan. If the conditions are right and your dough hasn't warmed up too much, it can often be folded into quarters, placed in the pan, and then unfolded. This works for both pies and tarts.

This is easier to demonstrate than it is to put into words, but here's what I do when I roll on parchment paper: When the dough circle is the correct size, I grab the left-hand side of the parchment with my left hand, then quickly lift it and almost simultaneously sort of flip the dough onto my outstretched right arm and palm, which I'm holding 6 to 8 inches above the counter. (I'm right-handed; lefties would do this in reverse.)

With the dough draped over my right forearm and palm, I very gently lower it onto my pan and carefully reposition it, so it's distributed evenly. Then I tuck the dough into the pan, lifting on the

overhang as I do this so I don't stretch the dough or make a hole in it.

An alternative method that I also like is to roll the dough directly on a lightly floured sheet of wax paper. The paper has just a little grip to it, enough that I can invert the rolled pastry over the pan, center it, then carefully peel the paper away from the dough before tucking it in.

A more straightforward way to get your dough into the pan is simply to slide the fingers of both hands under the dough, then lift it right in. Whatever works.

Some bakers like to roll the dough onto their rolling pin, then unroll it over their pan. You can try this if it sounds appealing, but it's my experience that the weight of the pin—and the fact that you're often left holding it with one hand while managing your dough with the other—makes this method feel pretty clumsy.

Shaping Your Edge

When our dinner pie is baked in a pie pan or tart pan, we like it to have an attractive edge. It doesn't have to be a work of art, mind you. And sometimes a good-looking edge just sort of happens on its own, as when the edge of a galette forms pretty pleats when you fold it over the filling. But even more important than a good-looking edge is one that simply holds its own and keeps the filling where it's supposed to be—inside the crust—especially when you're making a quiche.

If you use a 9½- or 10-inch tart pan (with 1-inch sides) for the quiche recipes in this collection, you should have enough excess dough to form solid, beefed-up sides that prevent leaks and hold plenty of filling. Assuming you've already tucked the pastry into the pan, and you have a nicely defined crease all around the bottom perimeter of the pan, take the

overhanging dough, fold it over (inward), and press it against itself and the sides of the pan. Press just firmly enough so the dough pushes up over the top edge of the pan by about ¼ inch. (See Tart Pans, page 9, for more details.) Refrigerate the tart shell, and when it gets cold and firm, gently pinch and sculpt the sides so the thickness and height are reasonably even all around.

When you're using a pie pan to bake your dinner pies, the process is different. Instead of folding your overhanging dough over and pinching it against itself, you will fold it outward and tuck it under itself to hide the seam. This isn't an issue with quiche, since the seam is always hidden by the filling. But with pies made in pie pans, the seam is up high and might show if you don't tuck the dough under.

As you fold and tuck the dough under, gently pinch and sculpt it to form what I typically refer

to as an "upstanding ridge," by which I mean a continuous, peaked mountain range, about ½ inch high, that runs around the rim. Once you've got that, put the shell in the refrigerator for 30 minutes or so, until the dough is colder and a bit firmer, which makes it easier to flute.

To make the flutes (or "ruffles"), shape the thumb and forefinger on one of your hands into a tiny V. Place the V against the outside of your upstanding ridge as if you were going to pinch it, and then, with the forefinger of your other hand, press against the V from the inside of the shell. Press gently, using just enough pressure to form a nicely shaped flute. Continue all around the shell, making one flute right after another.

Of course, you don't have to make these flutes—you can simply leave the upstanding ridge the way it is. But the flutes are easy to make and give your pie an attractive, professional-looking appearance.

Prebaking Your Pie or Tart Shell

With some dinner pies and tarts, such as quiches, it's important to prebake the shell. Prebaking the shell essentially hardens and seals it, making it much more impervious. Skip this step with a very liquid filling, and the moisture will seep into your bottom crust. It will end up flabby, and a flabby bottom crust—in lieu of golden-brown pastry perfection—will mark you as a pie-making hack faster than any other indiscretion you can imagine.

When prebaking is required, the recipes here will always instruct you to refrigerate your shell first, to firm it up. This coolness-induced firmness helps when you go to line your shell with foil, because a firm shell is more difficult to displace or get knocked around when you come in contact with it.

Once the shell is chilled, you want to poke the bottom of your shell 8 or 10 times with the tines of a fork. These holes will allow steam to release when you remove the foil, preventing the shell from ballooning up. Because these fork holes are small and tend to close up as the shell bakes, give the fork a very slight twist, after you've punctured the pastry, to enlarge the holes a little bit.

Next, tear off a piece of regular-weight (not heavy-duty) aluminum foil about 16 inches long, center it over the shell, and gently tuck it down into the shell so it fits the pastry like a glove, especially down in that bottom crease. It's important to get it into the crease because the shell tends to shrink up in that location. When that happens, it forms a curved surface that's prone to punctures if you're not careful. Compromise your crust, and your custard will run out.

When the foil fits the shell like a glove, fill it almost to the top with dried beans; bank them up the sides, so the walls are fully supported. Put the shell on the center rack of a preheated 375°F oven and bake for 25 minutes. Or, if you're using a removable-bottom tart pan, put it on a baking sheet first.

After 25 minutes, slide out the rack, grab the ends of the foil, and slowly lift out the beans. Slide the rack back in and continue to bake for 5 to 7 minutes more to complete the prebaking. This last 5 to 7 minutes is particularly important for the bottom of the shell, which, due to the weight and coverage of the foil and beans, typically takes longer to bake than the sides.

Incidentally, once you slide out the oven rack, the ends of the foil should not be so hot that you can't grab them. Even so, approach them carefully if you've never done this before. Also, if you're not comfortable with or confident about lifting the beans out with the shell still sitting on the oven rack, place your shell on a trivet on your work surface before lifting out the beans. Oh, and those dried beans? They can't be used for cooking now, but you can save them to reuse the next time you need to prebake a quiche shell.

At the end of that last 5- to 7-minute period, I usually just move the prebaked shell to a cooling rack. Sometimes, however, if I want to make sure the bottom crust is good and done—not fully baked, but no-longer-raw-and-even-starting-to-crust-over—I turn off the oven, partially open the oven door, and just let it sit in the oven for another 10 minutes. I find this to be a good practice if I'm using a ceramic tart pan, because the bottom takes longer to get crusty in such a pan. Then I move it to the cooling rack.

There's one final step you don't want to overlook when you're prebaking a shell that you'll be using for a quiche: plugging those fork holes. That's important, because your custard can leak through them and wind up on the wrong side of the crust. Not good. So here are a couple of suggestions: As soon as you take the shell out of the oven, place very thin shavings of a melting cheese over each group of holes. The residual heat will quickly melt the cheese and seal the holes. Or, after the crust has cooled, just plug the holes with a little cream cheese. Put a dab on your finger and swipe it across the holes, like you're plugging a nail hole with putty. Easy-peasy.

I like to let my prebaked crust cool off almost completely before I fill and bake the quiche, because the crust becomes even more impervious as it cools. But if you're in a hurry, just wait as long as you can before filling and baking.

DINNER PIE BAKING STRATEGIES

If you do any amount of baking at all, then you probably know, or at least suspect, that your oven is not the even-tempered appliance it would like you to believe it is. On the outside you've got a deceptive number of dials, knobs, and displays that would suggest you're the one in control. But don't be fooled: Your oven, like all ovens, is quirky and unpredictable. Several of mine over the years have had multiple personality disorders.

Ovens can vary wildly in the amount of time they take to preheat. They have hot spots and cool spots, and some recover more quickly than others when you open the door. Most electric ovens cook "drier" than most gas ovens do. The list goes on, but the point is this: Baking most anything, including dinner pies, requires you to stay on your toes, learn your oven's quirks, and make adjustments as required. Put another way, the oven leads, and you follow.

For instance, when I'm prebaking a pie or tart shell for a quiche, one made in a heavy ceramic pan, I like to at least start the prebaking low in the oven, because that's where my oven is the hottest. The quiche itself is typically baked in the center of the oven, the area where I can expect equal temperatures above and below my pan. But if I'm not pleased with the browning on top of my quiche, I'll move the quiche up toward the top of the oven for the last 10 minutes or so, where the more intense heat will do a nice job of browning. And I keep it away from the left wall, which seems to get hotter than the right one. Like I said, quirky.

My suggestion is this: Whether you're baking a quiche, pot pie, galette, or whatever, take notes. Write down the type of pan that you used, the oven temperature, whether or not you applied an egg wash glaze, and where in the oven you baked your pie. If you moved the position of your dinner pie during the baking, make a note of that, too. Lastly, were you pleased with the way it came out? Are there scorch marks anywhere? Write it all down. I can guarantee that creating a journal with these observations will make you a better baker, and one who gets more consistent, positive results.

Which brings us to our final and most important strategy: Just start baking. Dinner pie baking is a big subject, with lots of ground to cover, and the best way to become an accomplished practitioner is just that—practice. Pick a category you like, acquire any tools you need, and find a recipe you can't resist. (I don't think that will be too hard!) Be patient with yourself. Take your time and enjoy the process. Then gather family and friends around your table, and share your home-baked dinner pies with a world that's hungry for authentic, handcrafted sustenance.

PIE DOUGHS & PASTRIES

GO-TO PIE DOUGH

It's no mystery why I call this my "go-to" dough: It's so versatile that I use it for perhaps four out of every five of the savory (and sweet) pies that I make. You can't beat it for reliability, and it bakes up to a beautiful texture, perfectly balanced between flaky and short. This is the single crust recipe; the double crust version follows. The recipe calls for a food processor; to make the dough by hand, see the Note. **Makes enough for 1 (9½-inch) pie or tart shell**

8 tablespoons (1 stick) cold unsalted butter plus 2 tablespoons cold vegetable shortening (or 10 tablespoons cold unsalted butter), cut into ½-inch cubes

1½ cups all-purpose flour

1½ teaspoons cornstarch

½ teaspoon salt

2 teaspoons white vinegar

Scant ⅓ cup cold water

1 Put the butter and shortening cubes in a single layer on a flour-dusted plate, with the shortening off to one side of the plate by itself. Refrigerate for at least 30 minutes. Combine the flour, cornstarch, and salt in a bowl and refrigerate that mixture also. Pour the vinegar into a 1-cup glass measure. Add enough cold water to equal ⅓ cup liquid. Refrigerate.

2 When you're ready to mix the pastry, transfer the flour mixture to a food processor. Pulse several times to mix. Remove the lid and scatter about 6 tablespoons of the butter—a little more than half of the total fat—over the dry mixture. Pulse the machine five times—that's five 1-second pulses—followed by an uninterrupted 5-second run. Remove the lid and add the remaining fat. Give the machine six or seven 1-second pulses.

3 Remove the lid and loosen the mixture with a big fork; you'll have a range of fat clods, most quite small but a few larger ones as well. With the lid off, drizzle about half of the liquid over the mixture. Replace the lid and give the machine three very quick, half-second pulses. Remove the lid, loosen the mixture with your fork, and add the rest of the liquid. Pulse briefly three or four times, just like before. The mixture will still look crumbly, but the crumbs will be starting to get a little clumpier.

4 Transfer the contents of your processor to a large bowl, one large enough to get your hands in. Start rubbing the crumbs together, as if you were making a streusel topping—what you're doing is redistributing the butter and moisture without overworking the dough. (NOTE: If your dough mixture came out of the food processor more clumpy than crumb-like, don't worry. Just pack it together like a snowball, knead it very gently two or three times, and proceed to step 5.) You can accomplish the same thing by "smearing" the crumbs down the sides of the bowl with your fingers. When the dough starts to gather in large clumps, pack it like a snowball and knead gently, three or four times, on a lightly floured surface.

5 Put the dough on a long piece of plastic wrap and flatten it into a 1-inch-thick disk. Wrap tightly in plastic wrap and refrigerate for at least 1½ to 2 hours; overnight is fine. (You can also slip the wrapped dough into a gallon-size plastic freezer bag and freeze it for up to 2 months. Thaw overnight in the refrigerator before using.)

NOTE: To make the dough by hand, chill all of your ingredients as specified in step 1, but increase the flour to 1½ cups plus 1½ tablespoons. Remove the butter and shortening from the refrigerator 5 to 8 minutes before mixing; it should have a little "give" to it when squeezed between your fingers. Add about 6 tablespoons of the butter to your dry mixture; toss to coat with flour. Using your pastry blender, cut in the butter until the largest pieces of fat are pea-size. Add the remaining fat, toss to coat, and cut that in. The entire mixture should look like it has been "touched" by the fat, and nothing should be larger than pea-size. Pour half of your liquid down around the sides of the bowl, but not in any one spot. Mix well with a large fork, moving the mixture in from the sides and up from the bottom. Repeat with the remaining liquid, but add the last few teaspoons only if needed. Rub and smear the crumbs as specified in step 4 until a dough starts to form. Pack the dough and knead gently a couple of times. Flatten into a disk, then wrap and refrigerate.

Recipe for Success

In case you're wondering why there's vinegar here and in some of the other pastry recipes, it's because vinegar is an acid, and acids tenderize things made with wheat flour. That's why sour cream pancakes and buttermilk biscuits have that melt-in-your-mouth softness. Don't worry: You won't taste the vinegar in the finished crust.

GO-TO PIE DOUGH FOR A DOUBLE CRUST

This is simply a scaled-up version of the previous recipe, suitable for double crust pies. Remember that when you're preparing a double crust pie dough, always make one half a little larger than the other; the larger half is for the shell. If you are relatively new to pastry making, I suggest starting with the single crust recipe, even if it means you have to make it twice for a double crust pie (see Recipe for Success for my explanation). The recipe calls for a food processor; to make the dough by hand, see the Note. **Makes enough for 1 (9½-inch) double crust deep-dish pie or 2 large pie shells**

14 tablespoons (1¾ sticks) cold unsalted butter, cut into ½-inch cubes

4 tablespoons cold vegetable shortening, cut into ½-inch cubes

2⅔ cups all-purpose flour

1 tablespoon cornstarch

1 teaspoon salt

1 tablespoon white vinegar

Scant ½ cup cold water

1   Put the butter and shortening cubes in a single layer on a flour-dusted plate, with the shortening off to one side of the plate by itself. Refrigerate for at least 30 minutes. Combine the flour, cornstarch, and salt in a bowl and refrigerate that mixture as well. Put the vinegar in a 1-cup glass measure. Add enough cold water to equal ½ cup liquid. Refrigerate.

2   When you're ready to mix the pastry, transfer the flour mixture to a food processor. Pulse several times to mix. Remove the lid and scatter about 10 tablespoons of the butter—a little more than half of the total fat— over the dry mixture. Pulse the machine six or seven times—that's six or seven 1-second pulses—followed by an uninterrupted 6- to 7-second run. Remove the lid and add the remaining fat. Give the machine six or seven 1-second pulses.

3   Remove the lid and loosen the mixture with a big fork; you'll have a range of fat clods, most quite small but a few larger ones as well. With the lid off, drizzle about half of the liquid over the mixture. Replace the lid and give the machine three or four very quick, half-second pulses. Remove the lid, loosen the mixture with your fork, and add the rest of the liquid. Pulse briefly three or four times, just like the last ones. The mixture will still look crumbly, but the crumbs will just be starting to clump together. That's good.

4   Transfer the contents of your processor to a very large bowl, one large enough to get your hands in. Start rubbing the crumbs together, as if you were making a streusel topping. What you're doing is redistributing the butter and moisture without overworking the dough. (NOTE: If your dough mixture came out of the food processor more clumpy than crumb-like, don't worry. Just pack it together like a snowball, knead it a couple of times, and proceed to step 5.) You can accomplish the same thing by "smearing" the crumbs down the sides of the bowl with your fingers. When the dough starts to gather in large clumps, divide it in half, making one half—for the shell—a little larger than the other. Pack the halves like snowballs, and knead each one gently, two or three times, on a lightly floured surface.

5 Put the pieces of dough on separate sheets of plastic wrap and flatten each one into a disk almost 1 inch thick. Wrap snugly in the plastic and refrigerate for at least 1½ to 2 hours; overnight is fine. (You can also slip the wrapped dough into a gallon-size plastic freezer bag and freeze it for up to 2 months. Thaw overnight in the refrigerator before using.)

NOTE: To make the dough by hand, increase the flour to 2⅔ cups plus 3 tablespoons. Chill all of your ingredients as specified in step 1. Remove the butter and shortening from the refrigerator 5 minutes before mixing. Add 10 tablespoons of the butter to your dry mixture bowl; toss to coat with flour. Using your pastry blender, cut in the butter until the largest pieces of fat are pea-size. Add the remaining fat, toss to coat, and cut that in. The entire mixture should look like it has been "touched" by the fat. Pour half of your liquid down around the sides of the bowl, but not in any one spot. Mix well with a large fork, moving the mixture in from the sides and up from the bottom. Repeat with the remaining liquid. Rub and smear the crumbs as described in step 4 until a dough starts to form. Divide the dough in half, making one half slightly larger than the other. Pack the dough and knead several times. Flatten into disks, then wrap and refrigerate.

Recipe for Success

Less is often more when it comes to mixing pastry, and that goes for the volume of ingredients in your bowl when you're mixing. Simply put, a small batch of dough is easier to mix than a larger one. That's why, even though I give some double crust recipes here, I prefer the single crust ones. Your mixing will require less effort and everything will be more evenly mixed—without the risk of overworking the dough—when your mixing bowl isn't too crowded. This applies to both the food processor and hand methods. This isn't conventional thinking, and some will disagree with me. But that's the way I see it after many years of making—and teaching others about—pie pastry.

WHOLE WHEAT PIE DOUGH

There was a time in my life when almost every pie crust I made had some whole grain flour in it. I'm not as strict about it as I once was, but I still love the way whole grains add flavor, nutrition, and earthy hues to a pie crust. Here's my basic whole wheat pie dough, made with half white and half whole wheat pastry flour. The latter is milled from soft wheat, which yields a crust with a very tender, somewhat crumbly texture. (Indeed, without the all-purpose flour it can be too crumbly, which explains the half-and-half mix.) All in all, this is a delicious, versatile crust every pie maker should have in his or her repertoire. The recipe calls for a food processor; to make the dough by hand, see the Note. **Makes enough for 1 (9½-inch) pie or tart shell**

10 tablespoons (1¼ sticks) cold unsalted butter (or 8 tablespoons [1 stick] cold unsalted butter plus 2 tablespoons cold vegetable shortening), cut into ½-inch cubes

¾ cup all-purpose flour

¾ cup whole wheat pastry flour

2 teaspoons cornstarch

¾ teaspoon salt

⅓ cup cold water, plus another teaspoon or two if needed

1   Put the butter cubes in a single layer on a flour-dusted plate; if you're using the shortening, put the shortening off to one side of the plate by itself. Refrigerate for at least 30 minutes. Combine the all-purpose flour, whole wheat pastry flour, cornstarch, and salt in a bowl and refrigerate that mixture as well.

2   When you're ready to mix the pastry, transfer the dry mixture to a food processor. Pulse several times to mix. Remove the lid and scatter about 6 tablespoons of the butter—a little more than half of the total fat—over the dry mixture. Give the machine five 1-second pulses, then run the machine for 5 seconds uninterrupted. Remove the lid, add the remaining fat, then pulse the machine five or six more times, until the fat is broken into pea-size pieces.

3   Remove the lid and "fluff" the mixture with a large fork. With the lid off, drizzle about half of the water over the mixture and give the machine three half-second pulses to incorporate the water. Remove the lid, drizzle on the remaining water, and pulse again, just until the mixture forms clumpy crumbs that barely hold together. It should not ball up.

4   Transfer the crumbs to a large mixing bowl, then rub and smear the crumbs with your fingers until the dough coheres. Pack the dough into a ball. Using floured hands, gently knead the dough three or four times on a lightly floured surface. Flatten into a disk about ¾ inch thick. Wrap tightly in plastic wrap and refrigerate for at least 2 hours before rolling. (You can also slip the wrapped dough into a gallon-size plastic freezer bag and freeze it for up to 2 months. Thaw overnight in the refrigerator before using.)

NOTE: To make the dough by hand, chill all of your ingredients as specified in step 1. Remove the fat from the refrigerator 5 minutes before mixing. Add 6 tablespoons of the butter to your dry mixture; toss to coat with flour. Using your pastry blender, cut in the butter until the largest pieces of fat are pea-size. Add the remaining fat, toss to coat, and cut that in. The entire mixture should look like it has been "touched" by the fat, and you should have plenty of pea-size fat pieces. Pour half of your water down around the sides of the bowl, but not in any one spot. Mix well with a large fork, moving the mixture in from the sides and up from the bottom. Repeat with the remaining water. If your dough seems to need it, add another teaspoon or two cold water. Rub and smear the crumbs until a dough starts to form. Pack the dough like a snowball and knead briefly. Flatten into a disk, then wrap and refrigerate.

Recipe for Success

Whole grain flours are quite porous and can absorb more liquid than you might anticipate. Keep this in mind when you're mixing your dough and don't be alarmed if you need a few more teaspoons of water than is specified.

This dough, like most pie pastries, behaves better when it's cool, since the firmness of the butter is one of the things that makes the dough cohere. If your dough is cool but you're still running into problems with it holding together, it's probably because your flour is a bit coarse. Increasing the all-purpose flour to 1 cup and decreasing the whole wheat pastry flour to ½ cup should help.

CORNMEAL PIE DOUGH

I have always been fond of grainy pie crusts, and why not? They have their own unique flavor and texture, depending on the flour that you use. And they're a nice change of pace from the usual white flour crusts we make. This cornmeal dough is one of my old favorites, and the thing I love most about it is the slight bit of crunch: It's there, just barely, but enough so that people notice and say things like *This is good! How did you make the crust so tender and crumbly?* This works beautifully with all sorts of savory pies, but especially so with the Taco Pot Pie on page 164. The recipe calls for a food processor; to make the dough by hand, see the Note. **Makes enough for 1 (9½-inch) deep-dish pie shell or 4 pot pie shells**

7 tablespoons cold unsalted butter, cut into ½-inch cubes

3 tablespoons cold vegetable shortening, cut into ½-inch cubes

1⅓ cups all-purpose flour

¼ cup fine yellow cornmeal (such as Quaker)

½ teaspoon salt

¼ cup cold water

1½ teaspoons white vinegar

1   Put the butter and shortening cubes in a single layer on a flour-dusted plate, with the shortening off to one side of the plate by itself. Refrigerate for at least 30 minutes. Put the flour, cornmeal, and salt in a bowl and refrigerate that as well. Combine the water and vinegar in a 1-cup glass measure and refrigerate that also.

2   When you're ready to mix the pastry, transfer the flour mixture to a food processor. Pulse several times to mix. Remove the lid and add the butter cubes, dropping them here and there over the flour. Replace the lid and give the machine six to eight 1-second pulses, cutting the butter into small pieces (baby pea–size and smaller). Remove the lid and scatter the vegetable shortening over the mixture. Pulse three or four times, to mix.

3   Remove the lid and pour about half of the water mixture over the dry ingredients, but not all in one place. Give the machine two or three half-second pulses. Remove the lid, add the rest of the liquid, and pulse the machine again until the dough just barely starts to form large crumbs that hold together when you press them between your fingertips. Transfer the mixture to a large mixing bowl and gather it together, kneading it gently several times.

4   Turn the dough out onto a floured surface; knead two or three times. Place the dough on a large piece of plastic wrap, then dust it with flour and flatten into a disk about ¾ inch thick. Wrap in the plastic and refrigerate for 1½ to 2 hours before rolling. (You can also slip the wrapped dough into a gallon-size plastic freezer bag and freeze it for up to 2 months. Thaw overnight in the refrigerator before using.)

NOTE: To make the dough by hand, measure and refrigerate all of the ingredients as specified in step 1. When you're ready to mix the dough, transfer the dry mixture to a large mixing bowl. Add the butter; toss by hand to coat with the flour. Using a pastry blender, cut in the butter until it is broken into small pieces (baby pea–size and smaller). Add the vegetable shortening and cut that in also. (It will go quickly, since the shortening is so soft.) Push the mixture toward the center of the bowl. Add about half of the liquid, pouring it all around the sides of the bowl rather than in one spot. Stir briskly with a fork to dampen everything. Add the remaining liquid and mix again until the dough pulls together. Shape, wrap, and refrigerate as in step 4.

Recipe for Success

It's important to use a fine cornmeal in this recipe, not a coarsely ground meal. With fine cornmeal you won't have any trouble rolling the dough; use a coarse grind, however, and you may find that the dough becomes somewhat unmanageable and tear-prone when you roll it and lift it into the pan. With the brand I mention—Quaker—you get a consistent and uniform texture. In any case, make sure your dough is good and chilled when you go to roll it. That's another hedge against misbehaving dough.

TART PASTRY

Here's a buttery food processor dough that mixes up beautifully. (It's not a dough that's easily made by hand.) The pastry has all sorts of applications in the savory pie and tart realm. Among my favorite uses for this dough is the Creamy Red Potato and Parmesan Tart on page 86. **Makes enough for 2 (9½-inch) tarts or 1 large free-form tart**

1 cup (2 sticks) cold unsalted butter, cut into ½-inch cubes

2 cups all-purpose flour

¾ teaspoon salt

¼ cup cold water

1 large egg

1   Put the butter cubes in a single layer on a flour-dusted plate. Refrigerate for at least 30 minutes. Combine the flour and salt in another bowl and refrigerate that also. Whisk the water and egg in a 1-cup glass measure and refrigerate.

2   When you're ready to mix the dough, transfer the flour mixture to your food processor. Pulse several times to mix. Remove the lid and scatter the butter over the dry ingredients. Pulse the machine eight to ten times, cutting the butter into very small pieces.

3   Using the feed tube, add the liquid in a single 8- to 10-second stream, pulsing the machine continuously as you add it. Continue to pulse until the dough forms large crumbs that clump together, but don't let the dough ball up around the blade.

4   Turn the dough crumbs out onto a lightly floured surface and pack the dough into a ball. Knead gently two or three times, then place the dough on a large piece of plastic wrap. Flatten into a disk about ¾ inch thick. Wrap the dough in the plastic and refrigerate for 1½ to 2 hours before rolling. (You can also slip the wrapped dough into a gallon-size plastic freezer bag and freeze it for up to 2 months. Thaw overnight in the refrigerator before using.)

YEASTED BUTTER PASTRY

Most of the time, pie dough and pastry recipes don't have any kind of leavening, and when they do, it is seldom yeast. Here's one exception. This is a very easy dough to mix in the food processor. The kneading takes place right in the machine, followed by a quick hand kneading when you turn the dough out. It gets a partial rise at room temperature, with the second half of the rising in the fridge; the chill makes it easier to roll. Once baked, the texture of the crust is more biscuit-like than flaky pastry, so it's a good choice for many large galettes, especially those with a fair amount of moisture. I always use this for the Curried Winter Squash Galette with Onion and Apple (page 98), but it would also be great for the Fresh Tomato and Pesto Galette (page 81). **Makes enough for 1 large free-form tart**

½ cup lukewarm water

1¼-ounce packet (2 teaspoons) active dry yeast

2 cups all-purpose flour

½ teaspoon sugar

½ teaspoon salt

5 tablespoons cold unsalted butter, cut into ½-inch cubes

1 large egg yolk

1   Pour the water into a small mixing bowl and sprinkle on the yeast. Mix briefly with a fork, then set aside for 5 minutes.

2   Combine the flour, sugar, and salt in the bowl of a food processor. Pulse several times to mix. Remove the lid and scatter the butter over the dry mixture, then pulse the machine repeatedly, perhaps eight or ten times, until the butter is broken into small bits.

3   Add the egg yolk to the yeast liquid; blend with a fork. Remove the lid of the food processor and pour the liquid over the flour mixture. Pulse the machine repeatedly until the dough coheres. Once it does, run the machine nonstop for 8 to 10 seconds to knead the dough.

4   Turn the dough out onto a lightly floured surface; it will be a little sticky. Dust the dough and your hands with flour, and knead by hand for 1 minute just to smooth it out. Transfer the dough to a lightly oiled bowl, rotating the dough to coat the entire surface with oil. Cover the bowl with plastic wrap and let rise at room temperature for 30 minutes. Transfer to the refrigerator and let rise for another 30 to 45 minutes before rolling.

Recipe for Success

Even if you've never kneaded dough before, you can do this. Remember, the dough has already been kneaded in the processor; you're just giving it one last massage. Using moderate pressure, roll the dough away from you under one of your palms; the dough isn't big enough for two-palm kneading. Just scoot it along on the counter, keeping a little tension on it. Dust with flour if it sticks to anything. Lift the dough off the counter and repeat.

CHEDDAR CHEESE PASTRY

I love cheddar cheese pie crust. I use this dough for apple pies, but it gets a real workout in the savory pie department. It's excellent with just about any quiche or hand pie—you can get six good-size turnovers from this batch—but my favorite use might well be for the French-Canadian meat pie known as tourtière (page 186). **Makes enough for 2 (9½-inch) pie or tart shells or 1 double crust pie**

12 tablespoons (1½ sticks) cold unsalted butter, cut into ½-inch cubes

2 tablespoons cold vegetable shortening, cut into ½-inch cubes

2½ cups all-purpose flour

2 teaspoons sugar

1 teaspoon salt

1½ cups (lightly packed) grated extra-sharp cheddar cheese

1 egg yolk

Scant ½ cup cold water

1   Put the butter and shortening cubes in a single layer on a flour-dusted plate, with the shortening off to one side of the plate by itself. Refrigerate for at least 30 minutes. Combine the flour, sugar, and salt in another bowl and refrigerate that also. Put the grated cheese on a plate and refrigerate. Put the egg yolk in a 1-cup glass measure and add just enough cold water to equal ½ cup. Blend well with a fork, then refrigerate.

2   When you're ready to mix the dough, transfer the flour mixture to the food processor. Pulse several times to mix. Remove the lid and scatter the butter here and there over the dry ingredients. Pulse the machine six to eight times, cutting the butter into pieces no larger than small peas. Remove the lid and scatter the shortening and cheese over everything. Pulse five or six times, until the cheese is finely chopped.

3   Remove the lid and loosen the mixture with a fork. Drizzle half of the liquid (¼ cup) over the pastry mixture and pulse three times to combine. Remove the lid and add 3 more tablespoons of the liquid. Pulse again, just until the mixture starts to form large crumbs.

Rolling with Plastic Wrap

Many home bakers swear by it, but I typically don't roll dough between two sheets of plastic wrap. It's hard to argue with its dependability; dough simply won't stick to it. But I don't like the way it keeps crimping and needing to be readjusted when you use it on top of pastry. That aside, this cheddar cheese pastry can get sticky, especially if it's not good and cold, and if that happens to you then plastic wrap might be a good option.

4   Transfer the mixture to a large mixing bowl and see how it feels. If you find numerous dry areas, you may need to mix in the last tablespoon of liquid by hand. Otherwise, gather the dough, packing it gently, then turn it out onto a floured work surface. Divide in half, making them equal if you'll be using them as bottom crusts for two pies, or making one half slightly larger than the other if you'll be using them for a double crust pie. Knead each half several times and shape each into a ball. Place the balls on individual sheets of plastic wrap and flatten into ¾-inch-thick disks. Wrap in the plastic and refrigerate for at least 1½ to 2 hours before rolling. (You can also slip the wrapped dough into a gallon-size plastic freezer bag and freeze it for up to 2 months. Thaw overnight in the refrigerator before using.)

Recipe for Success

If you want to kick up the cheese flavor in this crust, use ¼ cup grated Parmesan cheese in place of ¼ cup of the cheddar. It really adds a nice kick.

When I use this crust for savory pies, I often add a teaspoon of dried herbs—like thyme or basil—for added flavor and visual interest. Just toss the herbs into the food processor right along with the flour.

CORNMEAL BISCUIT CRUST

This dough makes a few cameo appearances in the coming recipes, on top of a delicious chili cobbler (page 213), under and over a creamy tomato cobbler pie (page 210), and elsewhere. The preparation is similar to traditional pastry—mix dry, cut in fat, add liquid—but the outcome is clearly more biscuit than flaky pastry. As with the Cornmeal Pie Dough (page 28), one of the most appealing features of this crust is the slight bit of cornmeal crunch. I think you're going to like it. **Makes enough for 1 dinner pie or cobbler**

2 cups all-purpose flour

⅓ cup fine yellow cornmeal (like Quaker)

1 tablespoon sugar

1½ teaspoons baking powder

½ teaspoon baking soda

¾ teaspoon salt

5 tablespoons cold unsalted butter, cut into ½-inch cubes

¾ cup cold sour cream

⅓ cup cold whole milk

1   Combine the flour, cornmeal, sugar, baking powder, baking soda, and salt in a large bowl. Whisk well to combine, then refrigerate this dry mixture for 30 minutes.

2   Add the butter, toss to coat with the dry mixture, and then use a pastry blender to cut the butter into the dry ingredients until the mixture resembles a coarse meal, but with a scattering of larger visible butter pieces (no larger than small peas).

3   Whisk the sour cream and milk in a small bowl. Make a well in the dry mixture and add the liquid all at once. Using a wooden spoon, briskly stir the mixture until the dough pulls together. It should be a little on the stiff side. Let the dough sit undisturbed for 1 minute. Lightly flour the dough, your hands, and your work surface, then turn the dough out and knead it gently a few times. If you aren't using the dough right away, place it on a sheet of plastic wrap, flatten the dough into a ¾-inch-thick disk, then wrap in the plastic and refrigerate until needed.

Recipe for Success

A biscuit dough, especially one with sour cream, can be a little soft and sticky to handle. That's why I like to chill the dry ingredients before making this dough: As with traditional pie pastry, the chilling firms everything up and makes the dough easier to work with. If you can take the time to do so, I suggest chilling not just the ingredients to make the dough, but the dough itself before you roll it.

TENDER BUTTERMILK BISCUIT CRUST

Just about everyone loves a saucy pot pie with a crusty-soft biscuit topping of the sort this recipe yields. It's my favorite buttermilk biscuit recipe, and while you could bake the biscuits up separately, then split and place one on top of each person's filling, it's just not the same—nor does it have the visual *wow!*—as the complete package baked as one. Instead of cutting these into rounds, try slicing them into squares to give the top of your dinner pies a fresh look. My favorite dinner pie with these? Old-Fashioned Chicken and Biscuits (page 204), hands down. **Makes enough to cover 1 large dinner pie**

2 cups all-purpose flour

1 tablespoon cornstarch

2 teaspoons baking powder

1 teaspoon sugar

½ teaspoon baking soda

½ teaspoon salt

5 tablespoons cold unsalted butter, cut into ½-inch cubes

¾ cup plus 2 tablespoons cold buttermilk

1   Combine the flour, cornstarch, baking powder, sugar, baking soda, and salt in a large mixing bowl. Whisk to combine. Refrigerate for 30 minutes.

2   Add the butter to the dry ingredients. Toss lightly to coat the butter, then cut the butter into the dry ingredients with a pastry blender until the mixture resembles a coarse meal, but with some small pea-size pieces of fat remaining. (If time allows, refrigerate for 5 to 10 minutes.)

3   When you're ready to bake, make a well in the dry mixture and add the buttermilk all at once. Using a wooden spoon or large fork, mix briskly until a dough forms. Dust the dough, your hands, and your work surface lightly with flour. Turn the dough out onto the work surface and knead it very gently three or four times. Proceed as instructed in the dinner pie recipe. (If you're using this recipe for a dinner pie not found in this collection, typically the dough is patted a little thicker than ½ inch, then cut into 1¾- to 2¼-inch rounds, which are then placed gently on top of the hot filling. Baking time will vary, but about 25 minutes at 375° to 400°F is average.)

Recipe for Success

Refrigerating the dry mixture makes the dough easier to handle after you add the buttermilk. This chilling keeps the butter cool, which in turn makes the dough less sticky when you knead and pat it out.

PUMPKIN-SAGE BISCUIT CRUST

When you're in the mood for something other than a flaky top crust, these biscuits make a gorgeous variation for almost any saucy pot pie. They're the crowning glory for one of my favorites, the Vegetable Pot Pie on page 144. **Makes enough to cover 1 large dinner pie**

2 cups all-purpose flour

1 tablespoon sugar

2 teaspoons baking powder

1 teaspoon crumbled dried sage

¾ teaspoon salt

½ teaspoon baking soda

Pinch of ground cloves

6 tablespoons (¾ stick) cold unsalted butter, cut into ½-inch cubes

½ cup cold buttermilk

½ cup canned pumpkin puree (not pumpkin pie filling)

¼ cup cold whole milk

1   Combine the flour, sugar, baking powder, sage, salt, baking soda, and cloves in a large mixing bowl. Add the butter and toss to coat with the flour. Using a pastry blender, cut the butter into the dry mixture until it is well combined, with pieces of butter the size of peas.

2   In another bowl, whisk together the buttermilk, pumpkin, and milk. Make a well in the dry ingredients and add the liquid. Stir briskly with a wooden spoon until the dough pulls together. Flour the dough, your hands, and your work surface. Turn the dough out onto the work surface, knead it gently two or three times, then cut and proceed as directed in the dinner pie recipe. (Typically, the dough is patted a little thicker than ½ inch, then cut into rounds with a 2- or 2¼-inch biscuit cutter before being placed on the filling. It can also be patted out and then cut into squares.)

Recipe for Success

If you're wondering why there is sugar in a biscuit topping for a savory pie, don't be alarmed. The biscuits don't actually have a sweet flavor; there's not enough sugar for that. But there is enough to counter the bitterness of the leavening and add a bit more punch to the pumpkin.

When I say "knead" here—where you turn the dough out of the bowl—this is nothing like kneading a yeasted bread dough; that would be a sticky mess. Rather, use a very light hand, with light pressure, and treat the dough gingerly, keeping your surfaces floured. Do that, and you shouldn't have any sticking issues.

SAMOSA DOUGH

Samosas are little Indian appetizer pastries, commonly made with potatoes (as in the recipe on page 62), and seasoned with curry spices. This simple-to-prepare dough, modeled on a recipe by Indian cookbook author Julie Sahni, is what they're wrapped in. It has less fat and more liquid than other pastry doughs, and is kneaded briefly to give it some strength and durability for deep-frying. **Makes enough for 16 samosas**

1¼ cups all-purpose flour

½ teaspoon salt

⅛ teaspoon baking soda

4 tablespoons cold vegetable shortening, cut into ½-inch cubes

¼ cup water blended with 2 tablespoons plain yogurt or sour cream

1 Combine the flour, salt, and baking soda in a mixing bowl, one large enough to get your hands in. Mix with a whisk. Add the pieces of vegetable shortening and toss gently by hand to coat with flour. Gently rub the fat and flour together until well combined.

2 When all the fat is broken up, sprinkle about half of the liquid over the mixture and work the mixture with a large fork to combine. Continue to add liquid, a couple of teaspoons at a time, until the dough gathers together in a single mass. You may not need all of the liquid for the dough to cohere.

3 Turn the dough out onto a lightly floured surface and knead for 3 to 5 minutes, until smooth and supple. Shape into an 8-inch-long log, wrap in plastic wrap, and let rest at room temperature for 15 minutes before using. If you aren't making your samosas right away, go ahead and refrigerate the dough until needed.

FLAKY & STURDY HAND PIE PASTRY

I've been making hand pies for many years and I've yet to run across a crust recipe that's as reliable or easy to prepare as this one is. The first thing you'll notice is that the proportion of fat to flour is quite a bit less than your typical pie or tart pastry; that accounts for the "sturdy" part of the recipe title, sturdy being a desirable quality in the handheld dinner pies we use this for. But it's also flaky as all get out. The crust fractures into these lovely, large shards that will make you swoon. This pastry is so good, I use it for virtually all of my hand pies, and I almost always make it in the food processor. (If you prefer to make it by hand, see the Note.) **Makes enough for 4 medium-size hand pies or more smaller ones**

6 tablespoons (¾ stick) cold unsalted butter, cut into ½-inch cubes

2 tablespoons cold vegetable shortening, cut into ½-inch cubes

2¼ cups all-purpose flour

1¼ teaspoons salt

1 large egg

⅓ cup cold water

1 tablespoon white vinegar

1   Put the butter and shortening cubes in a single layer on a flour-dusted plate, with the shortening off to one side of the plate by itself. Refrigerate for at least 30 minutes. Combine the flour and salt in a bowl and refrigerate that as well. Gently whisk the egg, water, and vinegar in a 1-cup glass measure until combined and refrigerate that also.

2   When you're ready to mix the pastry, transfer the flour mixture to a food processor. Pulse several times to mix. Remove the lid and add the fat all at once, dropping it here and there over the flour. Give the machine six to eight 1-second pulses, cutting the fat into small pieces (baby pea–size and smaller).

3   Remove the lid and pour about half of the liquid over the dry ingredients, but not all in one place. Give the machine two or three half-second pulses. Remove the lid, add the rest of the liquid, and pulse the machine again until the dough just barely starts to form coarse crumbs that hold together when you press them between your fingertips. Dump the mixture into a large mixing bowl and gather it together, kneading it gently several times.

4   Turn the dough out onto a floured surface and divide it into four equal pieces. Knead each one a couple more times, then shape into balls. Put the balls on separate sheets of plastic wrap and flatten them into disks about ½ inch thick. Wrap individually in the plastic and refrigerate for 1 to 2 hours before rolling, or longer if desired. (You can also slip the wrapped dough into a gallon-size plastic freezer bag and freeze it for up to 2 months. Thaw overnight in the refrigerator before using.)

NOTE: To make the dough by hand, measure and refrigerate all of the ingredients as specified in step 1. When you're ready to mix the dough, transfer the dry mixture to a large mixing bowl. Add the fat; toss by hand to coat with the flour. Using a pastry blender, cut in the fat until it is broken into small pieces (baby pea–size and smaller). Push the mixture toward the center of the bowl. Add about half of the liquid, pouring it all around the sides of the bowl rather than in any one spot. Stir briskly with a fork to dampen everything. Add the remaining liquid and mix again until the dough pulls together. Knead, divide, and shape as specified in step 4.

Recipe for Success

The reason we flour the plate and scatter the fat around on it (instead of dumping it in a pile) is simply to prevent the fat from sticking to the plate or itself; the flour acts as a release surface. Keeping the fat in separate pieces also facilitates even mixing.

Just so you know, this dough feels a little moister to the touch than the Go-To Pie Dough (page 22) and others you may have made. That's just the way it is.

HAND PIES, TURNOVERS & PIZZAS

Kale & Smoked Chorizo Hand Pies   42

Chicken, Broccoli & Cheddar Turnovers   44

Tuscan-Style Pork Turnovers   46

Mini Mushroom & Goat Cheese Turnovers   49

Cornish Meat Pies   51

Baked Reuben Sandwich   54

Philly Cheesesteak Hand Pies   56

Spicy Chicken & Cheese Empanadas   58

Tempeh & Brown Rice Empanadas   60

Potato & Pea Samosas   62

Curried Chickpea & Rice Packets   64

Brunch Bacon & Egg Pizza   66

Stuffed Crust Phyllo Pizza   68

Eggplant Parmesan Pizza Tart   70

KALE & SMOKED CHORIZO HAND PIES

This hand pie is so delicious that I could eat one every day of the week (but that pretty much goes for anything with kale and sausage in it). It's like eating a little calzone and, as with the calzone, everyone seems to enjoy a little side dish of red sauce on the side, to spoon on each bite. Serve with nothing more than a big salad and you're all set. **Makes 4 servings**

1 recipe Flaky and Sturdy Hand Pie Pastry (page 38), refrigerated

FILLING

3 tablespoons olive oil

1 large onion, chopped

2 garlic cloves, minced

¾ to 1 cup beef broth

2 pounds kale, stemmed and chopped

8 ounces fully cooked smoked chorizo sausage, cut in bite-size pieces

1 plum tomato, halved, seeded, and diced

1 cup grated Parmesan cheese or 1 cup diced provolone or mozzarella cheese

1 egg beaten with 1 tablespoon milk

1   If you haven't already, prepare and refrigerate the pastry for at least 1 hour.

2   About 45 minutes before you want to assemble these hand pies, heat the olive oil in a very large skillet or stovetop casserole over medium heat. Add the onion and sauté for 5 to 6 minutes. Stir in the garlic and cook for another minute; salt and pepper the vegetables lightly. Add ¾ cup beef broth and bring to a simmer.

3   Add the kale, cover the skillet, and gently braise the kale for 10 minutes, stirring occasionally. Uncover the pan and continue to cook, stirring occasionally, until the kale is tender, 5 to 10 minutes more. (If there's too little liquid in the pan, add the remaining ¼ cup broth, or even more if needed, and finish cooking.)

4   When the liquid has mostly evaporated, stir in the sausage and tomato. Heat for 2 minutes, stirring often, then remove from the heat. Transfer the mixture to a plate and set aside to cool.

5   Preheat the oven to 375°F and get out a large baking sheet. Line it with parchment if you have some.

6   Working with one piece of dough at a time (and leaving the others in the refrigerator), roll it on a lightly floured surface into a round-cornered rectangle about 10 inches long and 8 inches wide. Draw an imaginary line across the center (crosswise) and put one-quarter of the kale and sausage mixture to one side of that line, leaving a border of ¾ to 1 inch uncovered. Cover with ¼ cup of the cheese. Press the filling down gently to compact it.

7   Using a wet fingertip or damp pastry brush, moisten the entire perimeter of the dough, then fold the uncovered half of the dough over the filling, lining up the edges. Press gently to seal, then roll up the border to form a sort of rope edge. Poke the top once or twice with a paring knife to let steam escape. Transfer the hand pie to the baking sheet, then make the remaining pies. Brush all four pies lightly with the egg wash.

8   Bake on the center oven rack until the pastry is a rich golden brown, 35 to 40 minutes. Transfer the hand pies to a rack and cool for about 15 minutes before serving.

Recipe for Success

Since the kale craze hit, I'm finding more and more varieties of kale in the market. I used to gravitate exclusively toward the common curly variety, but these days I'm quite fond of lacinato kale, also called Tuscan kale, which seems to be a little more tender and sweet. Don't be afraid to try different types when you come across them, but be aware that their cooking times might vary somewhat.

CHICKEN, BROCCOLI & CHEDDAR TURNOVERS

Broccoli and cheddar is a classic partnership—just think of broccoli-cheddar soup! Throw in some leftover chicken (or pick up a rotisserie chicken), and you have the makings of one fine dinner pie. As with several of our other turnovers, we add a bit of moisture to the filling, in this case with ranch dressing, which also contributes great flavor. If you want to try out a new dish on the kids, one with a low intimidation factor, this would be a good choice. **Makes 4 servings**

1 recipe Flaky and Sturdy Hand Pie Pastry (page 38), refrigerated

FILLING

2 tablespoons unsalted butter

1 medium onion, chopped

3 cups small broccoli florets

2 cups chopped cooked chicken

¼ cup chicken broth (see Recipe for Success)

2 cups grated sharp or extra-sharp cheddar cheese

¼ to ⅓ cup ranch dressing

1 egg beaten with 1 tablespoon milk

1 If you haven't already, prepare and refrigerate the pastry for at least 1 hour.

2 About 30 minutes before you want to assemble these hand pies, melt the butter in a large skillet over medium heat. Stir in the onion and sauté for 5 minutes. Add the broccoli and cook for 1 minute; salt and pepper lightly. Stir in the chicken and chicken broth and cook, stirring, just long enough for the chicken broth to evaporate and get soaked up by the solids, another minute or so. (You want to keep the broccoli on the crunchy side, as it will continue to cook in the oven.) Immediately transfer the mixture to a plate and set it aside to cool. Season with additional salt and pepper to taste, if you like.

3 Preheat the oven to 375°F and get out a large baking sheet. Line it with parchment if you have some.

4 Working with one piece of dough at a time (and leaving the others in the refrigerator), roll it on a lightly floured surface into a round-cornered rectangle about 10 inches long and 8 inches wide. Draw an imaginary line across the center (crosswise) and sprinkle about ¼ cup grated cheese to one side of that line, leaving a border of ¾ to 1 inch uncovered. Pile one-quarter of the broccoli and chicken mixture on top of that, then drizzle 1 to 1½ tablespoons ranch dressing over that. Sprinkle another ¼ cup cheese on top. Press the filling down gently to compact it.

5   Using a wet fingertip or damp pastry brush, moisten the entire perimeter of the dough, then fold the uncovered half of the dough over the filling, lining up the edges. Press gently to seal, then roll up the border to form a sort of rope edge. Poke the top once or twice with a paring knife to let steam escape. Transfer the hand pie to the baking sheet, then make the remaining pies. Brush all four pies lightly with the egg wash.

6   Bake on the center oven rack until the pastry is a rich golden brown, 35 to 40 minutes. Transfer the hand pies to a rack and cool for about 15 minutes before serving.

Recipe for Success

You could, if you want, skip the step where you add the broth to the broccoli and chicken. However, with hand pies especially, I like to build in a little extra moisture whenever I can. Just make sure you cook off any "loose" broth in the pan before you transfer the filling to the plate to cool.

TUSCAN-STYLE PORK TURNOVERS

I love these, and you and your guests will, too. First we brown some ground pork, then finely chop olives, sun-dried tomatoes, herbs, and feta in the food processor, and finally bring it all together in a delicate whole wheat pastry. These are exquisite party pastries, a show-stealing little nibbler that everyone will be talking about long after your soiree is over. You will be tempted to overfill these because the filling is so delicious, but resist the temptation or they'll be busting out at the seams. **Makes 14 to 16 appetizer portions**

1 recipe Whole Wheat Pie Dough (page 26), refrigerated

FILLING

1½ tablespoons olive oil

½ large onion, finely chopped

12 ounces ground pork

½ cup oil-packed sun-dried tomato halves, drained

½ cup pitted olives

2 garlic cloves, crushed

Small handful fresh basil leaves or 1 teaspoon dried basil

2 teaspoons chopped fresh rosemary or 1 teaspoon dried rosemary

1 teaspoon chopped fresh thyme or ½ teaspoon dried thyme

⅓ cup coarsely crumbled feta cheese

1 egg beaten with 1 tablespoon milk

1   If you haven't already, prepare and refrigerate the pastry for at least 1 hour.

2   Heat the olive oil in a medium-size skillet over medium heat. Add the onion and sauté until soft and translucent, 7 to 8 minutes. Add the pork and brown it thoroughly. Salt lightly and add plenty of ground black pepper. Remove from the heat and cool.

3   Meanwhile, combine the sun-dried tomatoes, olives, garlic, and herbs in a food processor. Pulse the machine repeatedly until the mixture is finely chopped but still textured; don't turn it into a paste.

4   When the pork is completely cooled, add it to the processor along with the feta cheese. Pulse the machine several times, just enough for the mixture to start clumping together. Again, don't overdo it—it should remain nicely textured.

5   Get out a baking sheet and line it with plastic wrap. Also get out a 3½-inch round cutter or something else that size you can use for a cutting template. Roll the dough out to a ⅛-inch thickness on a floured work surface. Keeping the cuts as close together as possible, cut as many circles as you can. As you cut, line the circles up on the baking sheet. If you need more space, put a piece of plastic wrap across the first layer and then make the next layer. You should be able to get 14 to 16 rounds out of the dough, perhaps a few extra if you overlap the trimmings slightly, press them together, and cut more. Refrigerate the rounds for 30 to 60 minutes.

Continued

6   When you're ready to bake, put everything in your work area: the filling, a little bowl of water to moisten the edges of the dough, and your rolling pin. Also have ready another baking sheet, preferably lined with parchment.

7   Work with one round at a time and keep the other rounds refrigerated as you work. Place the round on a lightly floured surface and roll it gently back and forth a couple of times to stretch out the length just a little, to about 4 inches or slightly more. This will make the dough more pliable and give you more room for the filling. Quickly moisten the perimeter with a wet fingertip.

8   Pick up the dough, letting it rest in one of your outstretched hands. Put a generous tablespoon of the filling right in the center, spreading it slightly from side to side across the width and leaving enough of a border so you can pinch the edges together. Now bring the edges of the pastry together so they line up evenly, then pinch to seal. Place the turnover on the parchment-lined baking sheet and repeat for the remaining dough and filling. When all the turnovers are filled, refrigerate them for 20 minutes and preheat the oven to 350°F.

9   Using a fork, crimp the edges of each turnover, or trim them ever so slightly with a pastry wheel or ravioli cutter, to make a decorative edge. (Or just leave them as is.) Brush very lightly with some of the egg wash. Bake on the center oven rack until golden brown and crusted, about 25 minutes. Transfer the turnovers to a rack and cool for 10 minutes before serving.

Recipe for Success

One of the things I like about turnovers and empanadas is how nicely they freeze, in case you want to make them in advance of your meal. Just prepare as usual, arranging them on your baking sheet. But instead of refrigerating them, place the sheet in the freezer. After about an hour, when they're frozen solid, wrap them snugly in plastic wrap and place in a plastic freezer bag. When you're ready to bake, arrange on a baking sheet and preheat the oven. Brush on the egg wash. They will take a few extra minutes to bake if frozen.

MINI MUSHROOM & GOAT CHEESE TURNOVERS

Everyone needs a few classy little tricks up their sleeve for a special dinner or party; here's one you can take to the bank every time. It's got hip and wholesome written all over it, and the combination of rich, butter-sautéed mushrooms and sharp goat cheese is a real winner in the flavor department. Maybe best of all, they can be made the day ahead and refrigerated, or wrapped and frozen for at least a couple of weeks, keeping pre-party stress to a minimum. **Makes 14 to 16 appetizer portions**

1 recipe Whole Wheat Pie Dough (page 26), refrigerated

FILLING

4 tablespoons (½ stick) unsalted butter

4 cups diced (¼-inch) white mushroom caps

1 large leek (white and pale green parts only), finely chopped (see page 130)

¼ teaspoon dried thyme

1 teaspoon balsamic vinegar

2 to 3 ounces goat cheese, crumbled

1 egg beaten with 1 tablespoon milk

1   If you haven't already, prepare and refrigerate the pastry for at least 1 hour.

2   Melt the butter in a large skillet over medium heat. Stir in the mushrooms and leek. Cover the pan, let it gather moisture for a couple of minutes, then uncover it. Add the thyme and salt and pepper to taste. Cook the vegetables until the liquid has evaporated, another 7 to 8 minutes; you should hear just the sizzle of the butter in the pan. Stir in the vinegar, mix well, and remove from the heat. Transfer the mushroom mixture to a plate to cool.

3   Get out a baking sheet and line it with plastic wrap. Also get out a 3½-inch round cutter or something else that size you can use for a cutting template. Roll the dough out to a ⅛-inch thickness on a floured work surface. Keeping the cuts as close together as possible, cut as many circles as you can. As you cut, line up the circles on the baking sheet. If you need more space, put a second piece of plastic wrap on top of the first layer and then make the next layer. You should be able to get 14 to 16 rounds out of the dough, perhaps a few extra if you overlap the trimmings slightly, press them together, and cut more. Refrigerate the rounds for 30 to 60 minutes.

4   When you're ready to bake, put everything in your work area: the mushroom mixture, the goat cheese, a little bowl of water to moisten the edges of the dough, and your rolling pin. Also have ready another baking sheet, lined with parchment or lightly greased.

Continued

5   Work with one round at a time and keep the other rounds refrigerated as you work. Place the round on a lightly floured work surface and roll it gently back and forth a couple of times to stretch out the length just a little, to about 4 inches. This will make the dough more pliable and give you more room for the filling. Quickly moisten the perimeter with a wet fingertip.

6   Pick up the dough round, letting it rest in one of your outstretched hands. Put a tablespoon of the mushroom filling and a little bit of goat cheese right in the center, spreading it slightly from side to side across the width and leaving enough of a border so you can pinch the edges together. Now bring the edges of the pastry together so they line up evenly and pinch to seal. Place the turnover on the parchment-lined baking sheet and repeat for the remaining dough and filling. When all the turnovers are filled, refrigerate them for 20 minutes and preheat the oven to 350°F.

7   Using a fork, crimp the edges of each turnover, or trim them ever so slightly with a pastry wheel or ravioli cutter to make a decorative edge. (Or just leave them as is.) Brush very lightly with some of the egg wash. Bake on the center oven rack until golden brown and crusted, about 25 minutes. Transfer the turnovers to a rack and cool for 10 minutes before serving.

Recipe for Success

Unlike the dough we use for empanadas, this turnover dough is much more delicate and well suited to the filling. The important thing, handling-wise, is to keep the rounds refrigerated while you work on the assembly. Once the dough loses its cool, it's much harder to work with. So, have everything you need staged in your work area before you begin.

   If you want to freeze or refrigerate the turnovers for an extended period prior to baking, don't apply the egg wash; that goes on just before baking. Arrange the frozen turnovers on your parchment-lined baking sheet, let sit for 10 minutes, then apply the glaze and bake.

CORNISH MEAT PIES

Observant cooks will no doubt recognize this pie as my take on the beloved Cornish pasty. That title, however, is both narrowly defined and protected by law, so I will steer clear of any feather ruffling and simply state that this meat pie is a variant, inspired by the original. It is, in essence, a meat and potato pie, often made with rutabaga in place of or in addition to the potato. It has few adornments or seasonings, which is why I will often add a squirt of Worcestershire, some thyme, and a good amount of pepper. I've been known to add a little A.1. sauce or even a spoonful of thick gravy if I have some around. Apparently, I've broken the rules just by sautéing the onion briefly; all pasty ingredients are supposed to go in the dough uncooked. In spite of my criminal misdeeds, I think you'll agree that this is one tasty meat pie just the way it is, or with some beef gravy on the side, the way some recommend. **Makes 4 large hand pies**

1 recipe Flaky and Sturdy Hand Pie Pastry (page 38), divided as instructed below and refrigerated

FILLING

3 tablespoons unsalted butter

½ large onion, chopped

1 medium carrot, peeled and finely diced

1 small russet potato, peeled and cut in ¼-inch dice

8 ounces sirloin steak or top round steak, cut in small cubes, or 8 ounces ground sirloin

2 to 3 tablespoons chopped fresh flat-leaf parsley

A few shakes of Worcestershire sauce or a little A.1. sauce (optional)

¼ teaspoon dried thyme

1 egg yolk beaten with 1 tablespoon milk

Meat gravy, to serve on the side (optional)

1   Prepare the pastry as instructed, but divide it into four equal pieces. Shape each piece into a ball, then flatten the balls into ½-inch-thick disks. Wrap the disks separately in plastic wrap and refrigerate for at least 1½ hours before rolling.

2   Melt the butter in a medium-size skillet over medium heat. Add the onion and sauté for 5 minutes. Stir in the carrot and potato. Remove from the heat and scrape the contents, butter included, into a large mixing bowl. Set aside to cool.

3   When the vegetables have cooled, add the beef, parsley, Worcestershire sauce or A.1. (if using), thyme, ½ teaspoon salt, and ¼ teaspoon ground black pepper. Mix to combine, then refrigerate until you're ready to assemble the pies. When you are, preheat the oven to 375°F and get out a large baking sheet. Line it with parchment paper if you have it.

Continued

4   Working with one piece of dough at a time (and leaving the others in the refrigerator), roll the dough on a floured surface into a 9-inch circle. Make an imaginary line across the center of the dough, then use one-quarter of the filling to make a compact mound just in front of that line. Leave a good 1¼- to 1½-inch border of uncovered dough around the filling on the filled side of the circle.

5   Dampen the entire perimeter of the dough with the egg wash, then fold the uncovered portion of dough over the filling, lining up the edges. Press to seal, then roll the edge of the dough into a rope-like border. Poke the top once or twice with a fork to make steam vents. Place the meat pie on the baking sheet and repeat for the remaining pies.

6   Brush all of the pies lightly with more egg wash. Bake on the center oven rack until golden brown and crusty, about 40 minutes. Transfer to a rack and cool for about 15 minutes before serving, with or without gravy on the side.

Recipe for Success

The late, great baking author Bernard Clayton tells the story in one of his books of how Cornish housewives used to tuck a spoonful of jam into one corner of the pasties they made for their husbands, who worked all day in the mines. The husbands would save this little "dessert corner" for the last bite. I've always loved that story, and have often imagined what a nice treat this would have been for a hard-working miner.

BAKED REUBEN SANDWICH

You love a good Reuben sandwich, right? Everybody does. But did you know that those classic Reuben ingredients—sauerkraut, corned beef, Swiss cheese, and Russian dressing—also stack up to a world-class *baked* sandwich? Here's the proof. It's all wrapped up in our always-reliable Flaky and Sturdy Hand Pie Pastry—trust me, you're going to fall in love with this dough if you haven't already—which, without all the usual bread, makes for a scrumptious Reuben that's a little lighter on the stomach. There's just enough dressing here to go *inside* the sandwiches, so it's not a bad idea to double the dressing ingredients so you have extra for dipping. **Makes 4 servings**

1 recipe Flaky and Sturdy
  Hand Pie Pastry (page 38),
  refrigerated

FILLING

8 ounces sauerkraut

⅓ cup mayonnaise

2½ tablespoons Heinz chili sauce

2 tablespoons minced dill pickles
  or pickled jalapeño peppers

½ teaspoon Dijon, yellow, or honey
  mustard

¼ teaspoon prepared horseradish

8 to 10 ounces thinly sliced corned
  beef, cut into ¾-inch-wide strips

2 cups grated Swiss cheese

1 egg beaten with 1 tablespoon
  milk

1   If you haven't already, prepare and refrigerate the pastry for at least 1 hour.

2   Preheat the oven to 375°F and get out a large baking sheet. Line it with parchment if you have some.

3   Drain the sauerkraut in a colander, then pick it up and give it a good squeeze to eliminate much, though not all, of the liquid. Transfer to a plate and set aside.

4   To make the dressing, mix the mayonnaise, chili sauce, pickles, mustard, and horseradish in a small bowl or a measuring cup. Add a touch of salt and pepper to taste. Set aside.

5   Working with one piece of dough at a time (and leaving the others in the refrigerator), roll it on a lightly floured surface into a round-cornered rectangle about 10 inches long and 8 inches wide. Draw an imaginary line across the center (crosswise) and put one-quarter of the corned beef to one side of that line; just lay it down in strips, leaving a 1-inch border all around it. Top the meat evenly with one-quarter of the sauerkraut, then dollop a generous tablespoon of the dressing on top. Cover with ½ cup of the cheese, then press lightly on the filling to compact it.

6   Using a wet fingertip or damp pastry brush, moisten the entire perimeter of the dough, then fold the uncovered half of the dough over the filling, lining up the edges. Press gently to seal, then roll up the border to form a sort of rope edge. Poke the top once or twice with a paring knife to let steam escape. Transfer the hand pie to the baking sheet, then make the remaining pies. Brush all four pies lightly with the egg wash.

7   Bake on the center oven rack until the pastry is a rich golden brown, 35 to 40 minutes. Transfer the hand pies to a rack and cool for about 15 minutes before serving.

Recipe for Success

In case you're wondering, all of the hand pies and turnovers in this collection can be scaled down if you're bringing them to a potluck or if they're part of a more comprehensive menu. Just divide the dough into eight pieces instead of four, make smaller (5½- to 6-inch) circles, and scale back the filling accordingly, using about half of what you normally would per turnover. A nice way to serve these is in a smallish, narrow basket lined with a napkin or parchment. Stand the hand pies on end and you have a nice, tidy presentation.

There's something of an art to squeezing the sauerkraut for maximum flavor and texture. If you squeeze it bone dry, you'll lose all of its tartness and moisture, and some of the flavor, so don't take it that far. Go easy and stop squeezing before you think you should. Taste it to check: There should still be a bit of tang and moisture.

PHILLY CHEESESTEAK HAND PIES

This is not, of course, an authentic Philly cheesesteak, but rather my approximation of what a cheesesteak might have been if its inventor had a thing for pastry instead of hoagie rolls. Besides, none of that will matter once you taste these portable pies because you'll be too busy stuffing your face and scheming how best to snatch what's left of your neighbor's unguarded portion. You'll notice that I've not included the oft-used cheese sauce in these—it's a bit messy—opting for straight cheese and some seasoned mayo, which provides all the creaminess you need. **Makes 4 servings**

1 recipe Flaky and Sturdy
  Hand Pie Pastry (page 38),
  refrigerated

FILLING

3 tablespoons unsalted butter

1 large onion, halved and thinly
  sliced

1 large green bell pepper, seeded
  and thinly sliced

8 to 10 ounces deli roast beef,
  thinly sliced (see Recipe for
  Success)

A few shakes of Worcestershire
  sauce

⅓ cup mayonnaise

¼ teaspoon prepared horseradish,
  or more to taste

Tabasco sauce

2 cups grated provolone cheese
  or a blend of provolone and
  mozzarella

1 egg beaten with 1 tablespoon
  milk

1   If you haven't already, prepare and refrigerate the pastry for at least 1 hour.

2   About 30 minutes before you'd like to assemble the hand pies, melt the butter in a large skillet over medium heat. Stir in the onion and bell pepper and sauté until the vegetables are soft and the onions start to turn golden, 10 to 12 minutes. Salt and pepper to taste.

3   Chop the roast beef coarsely into strips about 1 inch wide and add them to the pan. Cook, stirring, until the beef has browned, 3 to 4 minutes, adding Worcestershire sauce to taste. Remove from the heat and scrape the mixture onto a plate to cool.

4   While the mixture cools, whisk the mayonnaise, horseradish, and Tabasco to taste in a small bowl and set it aside. Preheat the oven to 375°F and get out a large baking sheet. Line it with parchment if you have some.

5   Working with one piece of dough at a time (and leaving the others in the refrigerator), roll it on a lightly floured surface into a round-cornered rectangle about 10 inches long and 8 inches wide. Draw an imaginary line across the center (crosswise) and sprinkle about ¼ cup of the grated cheese to one side of that line, leaving a border of ¾ to 1 inch uncovered. Pile one-quarter of the meat and vegetable mixture on top of the cheese, then dollop about one-quarter of the seasoned mayonnaise on that. Top with another ¼ cup of the cheese. Press everything down gently to compact it.

6   Using a wet fingertip or damp pastry brush, moisten the entire perimeter of the dough, then fold the uncovered half of the dough over the filling, lining up the edges. Press gently to seal, then roll up the border to form a sort of rope edge. Poke the top once or twice with a paring knife to let steam escape. Transfer the hand pie to the baking sheet, then make the remaining pies. Brush the tops of all four pies lightly with the egg wash.

7   Bake on the center oven rack until the pastry is a rich golden brown, 35 to 40 minutes. Transfer the hand pies to a rack and cool for about 15 minutes before serving.

Recipe for Success

While deli roast beef tastes great in these hand pies and saves a step, I realize that you may want to cook the steak yourself. You'll need an 8- to 12-ounce steak; choose any cut you like—sirloin, ribeye, top round, everyone seems to have their favorite. Freeze the steak for about 45 minutes, which will allow you to slice the meat very, very thin. Once the vegetables are done, get them out of the pan, add a spoonful of oil, then add the meat slices in a single layer and cook, stirring, until browned. Return the vegetables to the skillet, season to taste as directed, then remove from the heat and cool.

SPICY CHICKEN & CHEESE EMPANADAS

These delicious savory pastries fly off the platter whenever I serve them. (Which is to say, you may want to double the recipe.) Make the dough and filling the day before and they'll be a cinch to assemble when you're ready to bake them. **Makes 12 appetizer portions**

1 recipe Flaky and Sturdy Hand
  Pie Pastry (page 38), divided
  as instructed in step 1 and
  refrigerated

FILLING

2 tablespoons vegetable oil or
  unsalted butter

½ large onion, finely chopped

½ red bell pepper, finely chopped

2 garlic cloves, minced

2½ cups chopped cooked chicken

⅓ cup buffalo wing sauce

3 tablespoons mustardy
  barbecue sauce

1 cup grated extra-sharp cheddar
  cheese or pepper Jack cheese

½ cup crumbled blue cheese

3 ounces cream cheese, at room
  temperature

3 to 5 teaspoons whole milk

1 egg beaten with 1 tablespoon
  milk

1   Prepare the pastry, but divide it into twelve equal-size pieces instead of four. Shape them into balls, then flatten into disks not quite ½ inch thick. Place on a small baking sheet lined with plastic wrap; press another sheet of plastic wrap over them, covering tightly. Refrigerate for at least 1½ to 2 hours.

2   Heat the oil in a medium-size skillet over medium heat. Add the onion and bell pepper and sauté for about 7 minutes, stirring often, then stir in the garlic and chicken. Cook for 1 minute, then stir in the buffalo wing sauce and barbecue sauce. Cook and stir for another minute or two, until the chicken is evenly coated with the sauce. Transfer to a plate, then season the mixture to taste with salt and pepper. Set aside for 30 minutes.

3   Combine the cheddar, blue cheese, and cream cheese in a small mixing bowl. Mash well with a large fork until evenly mixed. Mix in anywhere from 3 to 5 teaspoons milk, to loosen the cheese and make it more meltable. Set aside.

4   Preheat the oven to 350°F.

5   Remove the plastic wrap covering the dough, but leave the baking sheet in the refrigerator. Working with one piece of dough at a time, roll it on a lightly floured surface into a thin oblong 5½ to 6 inches long and about 4 inches wide. Draw an imaginary line across the center—widthwise—and place a little mound of the chicken mixture just to one side of it; leave a ½-inch border all around the filling. Put a couple of spoonfuls of the cheese mixture on top of the chicken and press down gently to even it out.

6   Using a damp fingertip, moisten the entire perimeter of the dough. Fold the uncovered portion of the dough over the covered half. Line up the edges of the pastry and press them together; crimp with a fork. Place the empanada back in the fridge on the plastic wrap–lined baking sheet. Repeat for the remaining empanadas.

7   Transfer the chilled empanadas to a large baking sheet lined with parchment; poke the tops once with a fork to create steam vents, then brush very lightly with the egg wash. Bake on the center oven rack until golden brown, about 30 minutes. Transfer the empanadas to a rack and cool for at least 15 minutes before serving.

Recipe for Success

One of the tricks here is to roll the dough nice and thin, especially if you're going to use these for an appetizer, because thin pastry is light and delicate and won't taste heavy or fill anyone up. The exact dimensions that you roll the dough are less important than the thickness; roughly ⅛ inch thick, about as thick as a quarter, is ideal. This dough is perfect for thin rolling.

If you have extra dough around and you want to stretch this filling, stir in some finely chopped green olives or pickled jalapeño peppers.

I generally serve these on their own, but they're also great with some ranch or blue cheese dressing on the side, for dipping.

TEMPEH & BROWN RICE EMPANADAS

Here is a meatless take on empanadas featuring tempeh, a meat-like surrogate made from fermented soybeans. When the tempeh is simmered it becomes tender and porous, making it a good vehicle for other flavors and giving it the ability to mimic things like, well, traditional empanada filling. The brown rice adds bulk and whole grain goodness. Even hardcore carnivores, I'd wager, will be amazed at how much these taste like beef empanadas. (Email me and let me know if you agree.) If you'd rather use a different pastry than the one I recommend, the Whole Wheat Pie Dough (page 26) will give these an even more wholesome profile; see Recipe for Success. **Makes 12 appetizer portions**

1 recipe Flaky and Sturdy Hand Pie Pastry (page 38), divided as instructed in step 1 and refrigerated

FILLING

1 tablespoon soy sauce

8 ounces tempeh, cut into ½-inch dice

3 tablespoons vegetable oil

½ large onion, finely chopped

½ cup finely chopped red or green bell pepper

2 garlic cloves, minced

1¼ teaspoons chili powder

½ teaspoon smoked paprika

½ teaspoon ground cumin

⅔ cup tomato sauce

1 tablespoon barbecue sauce

1 cup cooked brown rice or other plain rice

3 tablespoons finely chopped pickled jalapeño peppers, plus a little of the jar juice if needed

¼ cup chopped fresh flat-leaf parsley

1 cup grated sharp cheddar cheese (optional)

1 egg beaten with 1 tablespoon milk

1   Prepare the pastry, but divide it into twelve equal-size pieces instead of four. Shape them into balls, then flatten into disks not quite ½ inch thick. Place on a small baking sheet lined with plastic wrap; press another sheet of plastic wrap over them, covering tightly. Refrigerate for at least 1½ to 2 hours.

2   Pour 1¼ cups water into a medium-size saucepan and stir in the soy sauce. Add the tempeh and bring the water to a simmer over medium-high heat. Reduce the heat, cover, and simmer the tempeh for 10 minutes. Drain, then transfer the tempeh to a plate to cool.

3   Heat the oil in a medium-size skillet over medium heat. Add the onion and bell pepper and sauté for 6 to 7 minutes, then stir in the garlic, chili powder, smoked paprika, and cumin. Cook, stirring, for another 30 seconds, then stir in the tomato sauce and barbecue sauce. Remove from the heat and set aside.

4   Transfer the cooled tempeh to a food processor. Pulse the machine until the tempeh is well chopped, but don't overdo it; you want the texture to be granular, not gummy. Transfer the tempeh to a mixing bowl and add the brown rice and chopped jalapeños. Add the sauce mixture and the parsley. Mix lightly, just until combined, adding salt and pepper to taste. If you like the flavor and want some additional moisture, add a few teaspoons of the pickled jalapeño juice. Set aside for 15 minutes.

5   Preheat the oven to 350°F.

6   Remove the plastic wrap covering the dough, but leave the baking sheet in the refrigerator. Working with one piece of dough at a time, roll it on a lightly floured surface into a thin oblong 5½ to 6 inches long and about 4 inches wide. Draw an imaginary line across the center—widthwise—and place a mound of the tempeh filling just to one side of it; leave a ½-inch border all around the filling. Top with a tablespoon of grated cheese, if you like; press down gently to even it out.

7   Using a damp fingertip, moisten the entire perimeter of the dough. Fold the uncovered portion of the dough over the covered half. Line up the edges of the pastry and press them together; crimp with a fork. Place the empanada back in the refrigerator on the plastic wrap–lined baking sheet. Repeat for the remaining empanadas.

8   Transfer the chilled empanadas to a large baking sheet lined with parchment; poke the tops once with a fork to create steam vents, then brush very lightly with the egg wash. Bake on the center oven rack until golden brown, about 30 minutes. Transfer the empanadas to a rack and cool for at least 15 minutes before serving.

Recipe for Success

Back in the day (the 1970s), when I first started using tempeh, I don't think it was common practice to simmer it first. It seems to be nowadays, however, and I think it's a good idea. I was initially concerned that simmering the tempeh would cause it to fall apart, but that's not the case. It remains solid, but still manages to soften up. Try it.

If you're using the Whole Wheat Pie Dough, the easiest thing to do is roll out the entire dough and simply cut it with a 3½-inch round cutter. Keep the cuts close together. The empanadas will be a little smaller, good for party-size appetizers.

POTATO & PEA SAMOSAS

These are the spicy triangular turnovers most of us know and love from Indian restaurants. I don't usually make deep-fried dishes at home, but I make an exception for these exotic little pastries because they're just so good. Surprisingly easy to make, also. Serve with your favorite sweet and sour chutney on the side. **Makes 16 appetizer portions**

1 recipe Samosa Dough (page 37)

FILLING

1 pound russet or red-skinned potatoes (1 large or 3 to 4 medium-small potatoes), peeled and cut into ¼-inch dice

¾ cup frozen peas (no need to thaw)

2 tablespoons vegetable oil

½ large onion, finely chopped

1½ teaspoons minced fresh ginger

1½ teaspoons garam masala

1 teaspoon chili powder

½ teaspoon ground coriander

½ teaspoon ground turmeric

2 teaspoons fresh lemon juice plus 2 tablespoons water

3 tablespoons finely chopped fresh flat-leaf parsley or cilantro

Several cups of vegetable oil, for deep-frying

1   If you haven't already, prepare the dough and set it aside, wrapped in plastic wrap.

2   Put the potatoes in a saucepan and add enough salted water to cover by an inch or so. Bring to a boil over high heat, then boil the potatoes for 5 to 6 minutes. Add the peas and boil until the potatoes are just tender, 4 to 5 minutes more. Drain the potatoes and peas in a colander and set aside to cool.

3   Heat the vegetable oil in a large skillet over medium heat. Add the onion and sauté for 6 to 7 minutes. Stir in the ginger, garam masala, chili powder, coriander, and turmeric. Cook gently for 30 seconds, stirring, then stir in the potatoes and peas. Stir lightly, coating everything well with the seasonings, then mix in the lemon juice–water mixture, the parsley, and salt to taste. Remove from the heat, transfer to a plate, and cool. Taste again, adding more salt as needed.

4   To assemble the samosas, divide the dough into eight equal pieces and shape them into balls. Place them on a sheet of plastic wrap and cover them with another sheet of plastic wrap. Lay out a third sheet of plastic wrap for your finished samosas. Working with one piece of dough at a time and keeping the rest covered, roll the dough into a circle 6½ inches in diameter on a lightly floured surface. Cut the dough circle in half. Using a wet fingertip, moisten the very edge of the straight side of one half. Fold this semicircle in half, lining up the straight edges, and press just the edges to seal. You will have formed a cone.

5   Cup the cone in one of your hands and spoon some of the filling into the cone, enough to nearly fill it but not so much that you can't seal it closed; see Recipe for Success. Moisten the exposed inside edges of the cone and press them together to seal. Set aside on the plastic wrap. Repeat, first for the other semicircle and then for the remaining pieces of dough.

6   When you're ready to fry the samosas, heat about 3 inches of oil to 350°F in a large saucepan. Line a baking sheet with paper towels. When the oil is hot, add about 4 samosas at a time to the oil—they should not be crowded—and deep-fry until golden brown, 5 to 7 minutes. Transfer to the paper towels as they come out of the fat. Cool for several minutes before serving.

Recipe for Success

The deep-fried pastry around the filling tends to mute the seasoning in the filling, so don't use a light hand with the herbs, spices, or salt. If you have fresh mint on hand, adding a finely chopped tablespoon will make the filling sparkle even more.

   This is one of those times when you'll be tempted to overfill the pastry so you have plenty of filling in each one. If you do, you'll find that there's not enough of a border left to create a good seal, and oil will seep into the samosas—or they may break apart.

CURRIED CHICKPEA & RICE PACKETS

Wrapped in phyllo and folded up like a flag, these spicy appetizer triangles are a cinch to prepare and bake up crisp and irresistible. The accompanying Yogurt Dipping Sauce is a match made in heaven. **Makes 12 appetizer portions**

2 tablespoons olive oil, plus extra for brushing the phyllo

½ large onion, finely chopped

1 or 2 garlic cloves, minced

2½ teaspoons curry powder

½ cup canned diced tomatoes, with their juice

1 cup cooked rice

1 cup rinsed and drained canned chickpeas

2 tablespoons chopped fresh flat-leaf parsley or cilantro

8 sheets phyllo dough, thawed if frozen

YOGURT DIPPING SAUCE

1 cup plain yogurt

1 to 2 tablespoons finely chopped pickled jalapeño peppers

1 tablespoon minced fresh mint (optional, but very nice)

2 teaspoons curry powder

2 teaspoons sugar

2 teaspoons fresh lime juice

½ teaspoon minced fresh ginger

1 Heat the 2 tablespoons olive oil in a large skillet over medium heat. Add the onion and cook until translucent, 7 to 8 minutes. Stir in the garlic and curry powder and cook for another minute, stirring often. Stir in the tomatoes with their juice, rice, and chickpeas. Cook, stirring, until everything is heated through. Add salt and pepper to taste. Remove from the heat and stir in the parsley. Set aside and cool thoroughly.

2 Preheat the oven to 375°F and get out a large baking sheet.

3 Unfold the phyllo sheets on a large cutting surface. Using a very sharp knife, cut each sheet lengthwise into three equal sections. Keep them close by in your work area, loosely covered with a slightly dampened tea towel.

4 Put one phyllo section on your work surface with one of the short edges facing you. Using a pastry brush, lightly brush the sheet with olive oil. Put a second sheet directly on top of the first and brush that one with oil also. (Keep the ones you're not using covered with the tea towel.)

5   Mound a heaping tablespoon of the filling mixture in one of the near corners, about an inch up from the short edge. Fold the opposite corner of phyllo over the filling, forming a triangle; the short, bottom edge should now line up with one of the long sides. Now fold this triangle up as you would a flag and continue to fold in the same flag-like manner until you get to the end of the phyllo strip. Brush the outside of the triangular bundle with olive oil and place on the baking sheet. Repeat for the remaining phyllo and filling.

6   Bake on the center oven rack until golden brown and crisp, 22 to 25 minutes; don't let them get too brown. As the packets bake, stir together all of the dipping sauce ingredients in a small bowl, then cover and refrigerate. Transfer the packets to a cooling rack and cool briefly before serving with the dipping sauce on the side.

Recipe for Success

This dipping sauce would also be perfect with the Potato and Pea Samosas (page 62).

BRUNCH BACON & EGG PIZZA

You often see this sort of dish prepared with pizza dough or those crescent rolls from a tube, but I think the idea works even better with a pastry crust. (Of course I would think that, right?) But really, when you take bacon and eggs and layer them on a flaky pastry with tomato sauce, bacon-sautéed onions, and cheese, how far off the mark could you go? Sticklers may argue that tomato sauce is a less than brunch-like element, and I would suggest they serve this for dinner. The eggs are added about two-thirds of the way into the baking, deposited into awaiting hollowed tomato slices. How well you cook the eggs is up to you, but there's something really irresistible about rivulets of runny yolk oozing over the bacon, tomato sauce, and pastry. Do some of the prep the day ahead—like the pastry—and this won't take long to assemble the next morning. **Makes 6 servings**

1 recipe Go-To Pie Dough (page 22), refrigerated

FILLING

4 or 5 slices bacon

1 large onion, halved and thinly sliced

2 large tomatoes

1½ cups favorite tomato sauce

6 large eggs

2 cups grated mozzarella cheese or a combination of mozzarella and provolone

2 tablespoons chopped fresh flat-leaf parsley

1   If you haven't already, prepare the pastry and refrigerate it for at least 1½ hours.

2   In a large skillet, fry the bacon over medium heat until crisp. Transfer the bacon to a plate and set aside to cool. Pour off all but about 3 tablespoons of the bacon fat, then add the onion to the skillet. Sauté the onion until good and soft, 8 or 9 minutes, then remove from the heat. Preheat the oven to 400°F.

3   Core the tomatoes and cut 3 slices, each ½ inch thick, from the center region of each tomato. Cut out the innards, so just the outer ring of the slice remains. Put these rings aside. (Discard the innards or chop and use to make tomato sauce.)

4   On a sheet of parchment or a floured surface, roll the dough into a large oval slightly less than ⅛ inch thick. Transfer to a large baking sheet. Spread the tomato sauce over the entire surface, leaving an uncovered 1-inch border all around. Fold the border up over the tomato sauce. Scatter the sautéed onions over the sauce. Place the tomato rings in a circle over the onions; they'll likely push up against one another. Put the pizza on the center oven rack and bake for 30 minutes.

5   While the pizza bakes, break the eggs into 6 individual little bowls or ramekins. (You want to do this now because you'll need to work quickly when you add them to the pizza.) While you're at it, put the grated cheese and bacon—coarsely crumbled—in your work area as well.

6 After 30 minutes, slide out the pizza and put it in your work area. Quickly slide one egg into each tomato ring. Salt them lightly, and pepper to taste. Sprinkle the grated cheese and crumbled bacon over the eggs. Slide the pizza back into the oven and bake until the eggs are done to your liking, 8 to 11 minutes. (Remember that the eggs will continue to cook even when they're out of the oven, from the residual heat.) Transfer the pizza to a rack and sprinkle with the parsley. Cool briefly, then slice and serve.

Recipe for Success

In the summer, I like to make my own tomato sauce for this pizza, using plum tomatoes and sweet bell peppers. A homemade sauce makes any special dish even more so.

If you want to show off the sautéed onions, instead of putting them on top of the sauce, scatter them over the eggs before you sprinkle on the cheese. This gives the top of the pizza a nice rustic look.

STUFFED CRUST PHYLLO PIZZA

In spite of my sometimes rocky relationship with packaged phyllo dough (see page 208), there's no denying that it's irreplaceable in a number of dinner pies, and a fine proxy in others, this pizza being a good example of the latter. To create this pizza, we layer the phyllo sheets in alternate directions, leaving a border on one side of each sheet that we stuff with grated cheese. The pizza is then topped with a quick sauté of onions, garlic, and sliced cherry tomatoes, along with a few other choice items like pesto, olives, and more cheese. It's a perfect matchup of flavors, on a crust that shatters into a thousand fine shards when you eat it. Not your traditional pizza experience, but a lovely one nonetheless. **Makes 6 servings**

2 tablespoons olive oil, plus more for brushing the phyllo

1 large onion, thinly sliced

1¼ cups halved cherry tomatoes or grape tomatoes

½ green or red bell pepper, cut in very thin strips

8 sheets phyllo dough, thawed if frozen

A little grated Parmesan cheese or dry Italian-style bread crumbs, to sprinkle between layers

2 cups grated mozzarella cheese

3 to 4 tablespoons pesto

½ to 1 cup sliced black olives or other favorite olives

½ cup crumbled feta cheese

1   Heat the 2 tablespoons olive oil in a large skillet over medium heat. Add the onion and sauté until it just starts to caramelize, 9 to 10 minutes. Add the cherry tomatoes and bell pepper strips. Sauté for 1 minute, stirring often; salt and pepper lightly to taste. Remove from the heat and set aside. Preheat the oven to 375°F.

2   Get out a large rimless baking sheet and line it with parchment paper, if you have some. Place one sheet of phyllo on the baking sheet. Starting around the edges, and brushing toward the edge—so you don't crimp the sheet—brush the entire surface lightly with olive oil. Dust the surface lightly with a little Parmesan cheese or bread crumbs. Lay a second sheet on top of the first one in the opposite direction; you'll have what looks like a stumpy cross. Brush that sheet with oil and dust as before. Repeat this process until you have all eight sheets of phyllo stacked on top of one another, alternating the direction, brushing, and dusting each time.

3   Scatter ¼ cup of the mozzarella cheese down the middle of one stumpy border. Fold the edge over the cheese, enclosing it, then roll the edge just a bit to make a rolled carpet-like edge. Brush this rolled edge with more olive oil. Repeat for the other three sides of the pizza.

4   Spread the pesto over the crust, then top with the sautéed vegetables and olives. Bake on the center oven rack for 15 minutes. Slide the rack out and top the pizza with the feta cheese and then with the remaining 1 cup mozzarella cheese. Bake until golden brown along the edges, about 10 minutes more. Transfer the pizza to a rack. Cool for 5 to 10 minutes, then slice and serve.

Recipe for Success

If you have plenty of cheese on hand, go ahead and use more of it in the rolled edge of the crust. You can never have enough cheese.

   As you can imagine, there's no end to the topping possibilities here. Instead of, or in addition to, these toppings, use fresh tomato slices, roasted tomatoes (see page 126), wilted spinach, pepperoni, sliced meatballs, different cheeses, etc. Just don't add too much weight, or you'll for sure be eating this with fork and knife. (You may want to anyway—it's pretty delicate.)

EGGPLANT PARMESAN PIZZA TART

This is—like the name says—essentially an eggplant pizza on a delicate, flaky pastry. Not that there's anything wrong with eggplant pizza baked on a yeasted dough. Hardly. But the pastry turns this into a more refined, fork-and-knife affair, dressy enough that you wouldn't hesitate to serve it for a sit-down dinner. And besides, some cooks just aren't into making yeast dough, but they'll knock out a pastry dough at the drop of a hat. Aside from all that, this is just plain good eating: I mean, really, how far wrong can you go with layers of tomato sauce, ricotta cheese, Parmesan, baked eggplant, and melted cheese on top? **Makes 6 to 8 servings**

1 recipe Tart Pastry (page 30), refrigerated

FILLING

2 large eggplants, sliced crosswise into ½-inch-thick rounds

Plenty of olive oil, for brushing and drizzling

¾ cup ricotta cheese

3 tablespoons pesto

⅔ cup tomato sauce

⅔ cup grated Parmesan cheese

2 cups grated mozzarella cheese

1   If you haven't already, prepare the pastry—squaring up the overall shape just a bit—and refrigerate it for at least 1½ hours.

2   Preheat the oven to 375°F and get out two large rimmed baking sheets. Line them with parchment paper, if you have some. Oil the pans or parchment generously with olive oil.

3   Arrange as many eggplant slices on the baking sheets as you can in a single layer. Brush them liberally with olive oil, then flip them over and brush the other side. Salt and pepper the eggplant, then bake for 20 to 25 minutes. The aim is to make them soft and relaxed. Leave the oven on.

4   On a large sheet of parchment paper, roll the dough into a rectangle that will fit your largest baking sheet; mine usually ends up about 13 x 16 inches, but the precise dimensions are less important than the thickness, which should be ⅛ inch or a hair thicker. Transfer the dough, on the paper, to the baking sheet (see Recipe for Success). Refrigerate the dough on the sheet for 15 to 20 minutes.

5   Combine the ricotta cheese and pesto in a small mixing bowl. Add a bit of salt and pepper and set aside.

6   Get out the pastry and smear the tomato sauce over the surface, leaving a 1¾- to 2-inch uncovered border all around. Next, dollop the surface with small mounds of the ricotta mixture, smearing it somewhat to smooth it out. Cover the sauce and ricotta with layers of slightly overlapping eggplant slices. Sprinkle the Parmesan cheese evenly over the eggplant. Drizzle the top with 2 to 3 tablespoons olive oil.

7   Using a spatula to help you lift the dough, fold the uncovered border of dough up over the filling; it will sort of pleat itself as you work your way around.

8   Bake on the center oven rack until the pastry is golden brown, 30 to 35 minutes. Slide out the tart and sprinkle the mozzarella cheese over the eggplant. Bake just until the cheese is good and melty but hasn't started to brown, 8 to 10 minutes more. Transfer to a rack and cool for 10 to 15 minutes before slicing.

Recipe for Success

If you're an experienced roller, it is possible to roll this dough on your counter and then lift it onto your baking sheet, but still a little tricky since the dough rectangle is so large. If you work quickly, so the dough stays cool, you'll have an easier time of it. Still, I prefer rolling the dough onto parchment and then lifting the whole shebang—paper and pastry—onto the sheet.

If you're baking this on the same sheet you baked the eggplant on, make sure the sheet is totally cool before transferring the dough to it. Otherwise, the butter in the dough will start melting, and that will alter the nice flaky texture of the dough.

LITTLE PIES, TARTS & GALETTES

Bacon & Tomato Mini Tarts   74

Tomato Tarte Tatin   76

Mini Hot Crab Tarts   78

Pepperoni Pizza Bites   80

Fresh Tomato & Pesto Galette   81

Little Roasted Tomato Tarts   82

Fried Green Tomato & Pimento Cheese Galettes   84

Creamy Red Potato & Parmesan Tart   86

Free-Form Zucchini & Tomato Tart   89

Savory Winter Vegetable Crisp   90

Kale, Potato & Ricotta Cheese Galette   92

Sweet Potato & Herb Parmesan Galettes   94

Cream of Collards Tarte Au Gratin   96

Curried Winter Squash Galette with Onion & Apple   98

Free-Form French Onion Tart   100

Colcannon Pie   102

Loaded Baked Potato Tart   104

BACON & TOMATO MINI TARTS

These little quiches make great party appetizers. We use a zesty threesome in the filling—bacon, sun-dried tomatoes, and goat cheese—but, as with a regular-size quiche, there's almost no end to the variations you can spin. Along with a great crust, the trick with any small tart is to get plenty of pizzazz in the filling with big-flavor ingredients. I discuss a few other ideas in the accompanying box, should you want to create your own show-stopping version. **Makes 12 tartlets**

1 recipe Go-To Pie Dough (page 22), divided as instructed in step 1 and refrigerated

FILLING

2 large eggs

⅔ cup half-and-half

½ teaspoon Dijon mustard

¼ teaspoon dried thyme

About ½ cup finely crumbled goat cheese or feta cheese

About ½ cup chopped oil-packed sun-dried tomatoes or roasted tomatoes (see page 126)

4 slices bacon, cooked until crisp

1   Prepare the dough, dividing it into three equal pieces. Flatten each piece into a ½-inch-thick disk and wrap the disks individually in plastic wrap. Refrigerate for at least 1½ hours. Get out a standard 12-cup muffin pan and a 3- or 3¼-inch round biscuit cutter and set them aside.

2   Working with one piece of dough at a time (and leaving the others in the refrigerator), roll it into a thin circle 8½ to 9 inches in diameter on a lightly floured work surface. Keeping the cuts close together, cut the dough into rounds with your cutter. You should be able to get four circles out of each piece of dough. Slide each round down evenly into a cup, pushing it gently so you don't stretch it. The dough should have a nicely defined (not rounded off) crease around the bottom perimeter of the cup. Repeat, lining the rest of the cups. Refrigerate the muffin pan for at least 30 minutes. (Gather your scraps and press together. Wrap well, freeze, and use later to make a small pie.) Meanwhile, preheat the oven to 350°F.

3   Whisk the eggs in a mixing bowl until evenly blended; I like to use a spouted bowl for this because you can pour right into the cups. Whisk in the half-and-half, mustard, thyme, ¼ teaspoon salt, and ground black pepper to taste. Set aside.

Little Tarts, Lots of Options

Think of this recipe as a jumping-off point for building customized mini quiches of your own design. Pantry items with big, concentrated flavors are always a good place to start, including full-flavored cheeses, salty olives, pesto, smoked sausages, even pickled vegetables. Caramelized onions bring deep flavor, as do sautéed spinach, asparagus tips, and broccoli florets. Chop everything well, fill the cups loosely with your tidbits, then pour in enough custard—using the same one here—to just barely fill the shells. Bake as instructed and let the party begin.

4   Get out the chilled muffin pan. Put a little bit of the crumbled cheese and chopped tomato in each shell, dividing them equally among the cups. Whisk the custard again, then pour or ladle enough custard into each shell to almost reach the top. Don't go over the top edge or the custard will spill and make the tarts difficult to remove. Crumble a little bacon on top of each one.

5   Bake the tarts on the center oven rack until they've puffed up and the edge of the pastry is golden, about 25 minutes. Transfer the pan to a rack and cool for 10 minutes. Run a knife around each one, then lift out the tarts and serve as soon as possible.

Recipe for Success

Be sure to use a cutter that's at least 3 inches in diameter but no more than 3¼ inches. Smaller, and they'll hold too little filling; bigger, and they start to become too unwieldy for an appetizer.

For this recipe, as well as the Pepperoni Pizza Bites and the Mini Hot Crab Tarts recipes, you have the option of using another pastry I quite like: the Flaky and Sturdy Hand Pie Pastry on page 38. It's a little less flaky and delicate than the Go-To Pie Dough, and some folks like the extra durability for handheld food. Just know that the hand pie pastry dough recipe is larger, so you'll need only two-thirds to three-quarters of it to make a dozen tarts. Or, of course, you can simply prepare more filling and use all of it to make extra tarts.

TOMATO TARTE TATIN

You've probably heard of *tarte tatin*, the French dessert of caramelized apples (or sometimes pears). The tart is baked in a skillet with the pastry on top, then inverted onto a plate and served fruit side up. You may be surprised—and delighted—to learn that this idea translates nicely into a savory tomato version. Roma tomatoes are ideal because they're meatier and less watery than other tomatoes, so they hold up better in the skillet. **Makes 6 to 8 servings**

1 recipe Go-To Pie Dough (page 22), refrigerated

FILLING

10 to 12 large plum tomatoes

4 tablespoons (½ stick) unsalted butter

½ cup finely chopped onion

1½ tablespoons packed light brown sugar

1½ tablespoons balsamic vinegar

⅓ cup grated Parmesan cheese

1   If you haven't already, prepare the pastry and refrigerate it for at least 1½ hours.

2   Core and then halve the tomatoes lengthwise. Using a finger, push out the seeds from each half, doing a pretty thorough job of it—you don't want excess moisture in the skillet. Set the tomatoes aside.

3   Select a large, nonreactive oven-going skillet; an all-stainless-steel skillet is good, or use a nonstick skillet with an ovensafe handle. Melt the butter over medium heat. Stir in the onion and sauté for 5 minutes. Stir in the brown sugar and vinegar and immediately add the tomatoes, cut sides down, packing them as close together as possible. When they're all in the pan, cook for 1 minute. Using tongs, turn the tomatoes over and cook for 1 minute more, but no longer. Remove from the heat. Salt and pepper the tomatoes; don't skimp on either. Cool for 20 minutes, then sprinkle the Parmesan cheese over the tomatoes. Meanwhile, preheat the oven to 375°F.

4   After 20 minutes, roll the pastry into a 12-inch circle on a lightly floured sheet of wax paper. Invert the pastry over the tomatoes, center it, then peel off the paper. Tuck any excess pastry down the sides of the skillet. Using a large fork or the tip of a paring knife, poke one or two steam vents in the top.

5   Bake the tart on the center oven rack until the pastry is golden brown and the tomatoes are bubbly around the edge, about 30 minutes. Transfer the skillet to a cooling rack and cool for 5 to 10 minutes.

6   Gently place a plate (or the removable bottom of a tart pan) upside-down over the pastry. With oven mitts and long sleeves to protect your arms from hot juice that could leak out, secure the plate and flip the tart over. Remove the pan. If any tomatoes stick to the pan, simply put them back on the tart. Slice and serve.

Recipe for Success

I've also made this tart with half zucchini and half tomatoes and it's quite good. Use about 8 tomatoes and 1 medium or 2 small zucchini, cut into ½-inch-thick rounds. Follow the same steps as directed, alternating zucchini rounds with the tomatoes.

Don't wait much longer than 10 minutes to remove the tart from the pan, or the glaze will begin to thicken and the tomatoes may stick. Expect a little bit of juiciness on the pastry when you serve this.

MINI HOT CRAB TARTS

You've had hot crab dip before; this is hot crab dip in your own private pastry, a delectable little two- or three-bite nibbler that's the perfect party appetizer. Not only do these taste incredible, they can be made a day or two ahead and refrigerated. Just arrange them on a baking sheet and reheat for about 10 minutes in a 300°F oven just prior to serving. This recipe makes enough for a small gathering, but for a larger one you'll want to double the recipe. **Makes 12 tartlets**

1 recipe Go-To Pie Dough (page 22), divided as instructed in step 1 and refrigerated

FILLING

1 tablespoon unsalted butter

½ cup finely chopped onion

1 garlic clove, minced

½ teaspoon Old Bay Seasoning or other seafood seasoning

4 ounces cream cheese, at room temperature

¼ cup mayonnaise

3 tablespoons sour cream

1 tablespoon finely chopped pickled jalapeño peppers, plus a little of the pickling juice

½ teaspoon Dijon mustard

½ teaspoon Worcestershire sauce

5 ounces drained and flaked canned crabmeat

1 cup grated sharp or extra-sharp cheddar cheese

1   Prepare the dough, dividing it into three equal pieces. Flatten each piece into a ½-inch-thick disk and wrap the disks individually in plastic wrap. Refrigerate for at least 1½ hours. Get out a standard 12-cup muffin pan and a 3- or 3¼-inch round biscuit cutter and set them aside.

2   Working with one piece of dough at a time (and leaving the others in the refrigerator), roll it into a thin circle 8½ to 9 inches in diameter on a lightly floured work surface. Keeping the cuts close together, cut the dough into rounds with your biscuit cutter. You should be able to get four circles out of each piece of dough. Slide each round down evenly into a muffin cup, pushing it gently so you don't stretch it. The dough should have a nicely defined (not rounded off) crease around the bottom perimeter of the cup. Repeat with the other two pieces of dough, lining the rest of the cups. Refrigerate the muffin pan. (Gather your scraps and press together. Wrap well, freeze, and use later to make a small pie.)

3   While the shells chill, make the filling. Melt the butter in a small skillet over medium heat and add the onion. Sauté gently for 7 to 8 minutes, stirring in the garlic and seafood seasoning right at the end. Remove from the heat and set aside.

4   Using an electric mixer, gently beat the cream cheese, mayonnaise, and sour cream until smooth. Blend in the chopped jalapeños, 2 to 3 teaspoons of the jalapeño juice, the mustard, and the Worcestershire sauce. Add the onion mixture, scraping the pan well to get out all the seasoning. Using a wooden spoon, stir in the crabmeat, cheddar cheese, ¼ teaspoon salt, and ground black pepper to taste; stir until evenly mixed. Cover and refrigerate for 30 minutes. Meanwhile, preheat the oven to 375°F.

5   Divide the filling among the shells, smoothing the tops. Bake until slightly puffed and golden, 22 to 25 minutes. Transfer the pan to a rack and cool for 10 to 15 minutes. Run a spoon around each tart to loosen, then lift them out and let them cool a bit more on the rack. These are best served warm and can easily be reheated on a baking sheet in a moderate oven for 10 minutes. *Do not microwave.*

Recipe for Success

Working quickly with the cut dough, and keeping it cool, will help quite a bit with getting the rounds down into the cups successfully. Especially when the weather is warm, I'll roll out all three pieces of the dough, stack the pieces between sheets of plastic wrap, and refrigerate them for 30 to 60 minutes before cutting. The dough will cut much cleaner this way, and it will have less tendency to stretch when you nudge it down into the muffin cups.

PEPPERONI PIZZA BITES

Everyone loves pizza, but it's a bit out of its element at a more formal get-together. These pastry pizza bites are the perfect solution: the dish everyone digs, only dressed up for the occasion. We again use our go-to dough for the crust, then top it with tomato sauce, olives, pepperoni, and cheese. (I often add a bit of chopped sun-dried tomato for an even deeper tomato flavor.) These reheat beautifully. Just arrange on a baking sheet and place in a 300°F oven for 10 minutes. *Do not microwave.* **Makes 12 tartlets**

1 recipe Go-To Pie Dough (page 22), divided as instructed in step 1 and refrigerated

FILLING

¾ cup favorite thick and full-flavored tomato sauce

¼ cup slivered oil-packed sun-dried tomatoes (optional)

½ to ¾ cup finely chopped pepperoni

½ cup finely chopped pitted black olives

½ to ¾ cup finely diced mozzarella cheese

1   Prepare the dough, dividing it into three equal pieces. Flatten each piece into a ½-inch-thick disk and wrap the disks individually in plastic wrap. Refrigerate for at least 1½ hours. Get out a standard 12-cup muffin pan and a 3- or 3¼-inch round biscuit cutter and set them aside.

2   Working with one piece of dough at a time (and leaving the others in the refrigerator), roll it into a circle 8½ to 9 inches in diameter on a lightly floured work surface. Keeping the cuts close together, cut the dough into rounds with your cutter. You should be able to get four circles out of each piece of dough. Slide each round down evenly into a cup, pushing it in gently so you don't stretch it. The dough should have a nicely defined (not rounded off) crease around the bottom perimeter of the cup. Repeat, lining the rest of the cups. Refrigerate the muffin pan for at least 30 minutes. (Gather your scraps and press together. Wrap well, freeze, and use later to make a small pie.) Meanwhile, preheat the oven to 375°F.

3   Get out the chilled shells and spoon about a teaspoon of tomato sauce into each shell. Place a little bit of sun-dried tomato on top, if you like. Top with more or less equal parts pepperoni, olives, and cheese, going a little heavier on the cheese. You can mound the ingredients slightly, but keep the mounded part toward the middle of the shell.

4   Bake on the center oven rack until the little pizzas are golden brown, 22 to 25 minutes. Transfer the pan to a rack and cool for about 10 minutes. Run a knife around each one to loosen, and remove from the pan. Serve as soon as possible, or cool and wrap the pizzas and store in the refrigerator for up to 2 days.

FRESH TOMATO & PESTO GALETTE

This gorgeous summer galette is topped with a mixture of ricotta, Parmesan, and pesto, then covered with sliced fresh tomatoes. It makes a beautiful focal point for a breezy summer supper, accompanied by a seasonal salad. Perfect for the vegetarians at your table. **Makes 6 to 8 servings**

1 recipe Go-To Pie Dough (page 22), refrigerated

FILLING

¾ cup ricotta cheese

½ cup grated Parmesan cheese

¼ cup pesto or finely chopped fresh basil

1 tablespoon heavy cream, half-and-half, or whole milk

3 or 4 medium tomatoes, cored and thinly sliced

Handful of pitted black olives, sliced (optional)

1   If you haven't already, prepare the pastry and refrigerate it for at least 1½ hours.

2   While the dough chills, combine the ricotta cheese, about two-thirds of the Parmesan cheese, and the pesto in a small bowl. Stir to blend, adding salt and pepper to taste. Stir in the cream to smooth it out. Set aside. Preheat the oven to 375°F.

3   Roll the dough into a circle about 13 inches in diameter on a lightly floured surface. Transfer the dough to a large rimless baking sheet. (Even easier: Roll the dough on a large sheet of parchment paper and slide the parchment and dough right onto the sheet.)

4   Smear the cheese mixture evenly over the dough, leaving an uncovered border of about 1½ inches all around. Cover the cheese with slightly overlapping slices of tomato. If the tomatoes are very juicy, you may want to push the pulp and seeds out of an occasional slice, so you don't end up with an excess of liquid. Lightly salt and pepper the tomatoes. Using a dough scraper to help you lift, fold the uncovered border of dough up over the outer row of tomatoes. The dough will sort of pleat itself as you do so.

5   Place the galette on the center oven rack and bake until golden brown, about 45 minutes, turning the baking sheet 180 degrees after about 20 minutes. Transfer the baking sheet to a cooling rack and immediately sprinkle the top of the galette with the olives, if you are using them, and the remaining Parmesan cheese. Cool for 5 to 10 minutes before serving.

Recipe for Success

If you want the edge of the galette to have a shiny, dark golden finish, lightly brush the exposed border with egg wash—1 egg yolk beaten with 1 tablespoon milk—just before the galette goes in the oven.

LITTLE ROASTED TOMATO TARTS

These tarts are meant to be eaten warm, and they're just saucy enough to require that you make them individually, to fully contain the luscious tomato creaminess. As far as tomato tarts go, these are hard to top. Roasting the tomatoes—for maximum flavor—gives you a leg up on the competition right off the bat; adding layers of Parmesan and heavy cream makes it difficult to find the right superlatives. Don't bother making these unless it's tomato season where you live. **Makes 6 servings**

1 recipe Go-To Pie Dough (page 22), divided as instructed in step 1 and refrigerated

FILLING

2 to 3 tablespoons cornmeal

1½ to 2 pounds roasted tomatoes (see page 126)

¾ to 1 cup grated Parmesan cheese

1 cup heavy cream or whipping cream

1   Prepare the pastry as instructed, but divide it into six equal balls. Flatten the balls into ½-inch-thick disks, place them on a plate, and refrigerate for 1 to 1½ hours. Get out six shallow individual pie plates measuring 4½ to 5 inches in diameter.

2   Working with one piece of dough at a time (and leaving the others in the refrigerator), roll it into a thin circle 6½ to 7 inches in diameter on a lightly floured surface. Line a pie plate with the dough. Roll the overhanging dough back to form a rope edge, then pinch it into an upstanding ridge. Make a ruffled edge, if desired. Transfer to the refrigerator, then repeat for the remaining dough and pie plates. Refrigerate for 1 hour.

3   When you're ready to bake, preheat the oven to 375°F. Get out a baking sheet large enough to hold all of the pie plates.

4   Put all of the pie shells on your work surface and sprinkle ½ teaspoon cornmeal evenly in each one. Add a single, tightly packed layer of tomato slices; dust with more cornmeal, and add salt and pepper to taste. Top with 1 to 1½ tablespoons Parmesan cheese and about 1½ tablespoons cream. Repeat the layering one more time—tomato slices; a dusting of cornmeal, salt, and pepper; and finally the cheese and cream.

5   Bake the tarts on the center oven rack until the tops are golden and the filling is bubbly, 35 to 40 minutes. Transfer to a rack and cool for at least 20 minutes before serving. These are best eaten warm.

FRIED GREEN TOMATO & PIMENTO CHEESE GALETTES

Down South, we use a lot of green tomatoes and pimento cheese, separately and—on occasion, as here—together. You will need to make the pimento cheese ahead of time, which itself could be a real revelation to you if you're not already a believer (see Recipe for Success). Once that's done, all that's left is to fry up your green tomatoes, roll your pastry, and assemble the tart. If you're entertaining friends from the South, or you're lucky enough to already live here, I promise that you'll take an immediate shine to this cheesy, down-home concoction. One galette serves two as a main course, with a salad on the side. **Makes 6 servings**

1 recipe Go-To Pie Dough (page 22), divided as instructed in step 1 and refrigerated

PIMENTO CHEESE

8 ounces extra-sharp white cheddar cheese, grated

8 ounces mild or medium-sharp orange cheddar cheese, grated

⅔ cup mayonnaise

3 ounces cream cheese, softened

1 teaspoon Worcestershire sauce

⅛ to ¼ teaspoon cayenne pepper

1 (4-ounce) jar pimentos, drained and chopped

FILLING

1½ tablespoons vegetable oil

5 slices thick-cut bacon, cut into ½-inch pieces

½ large onion, chopped

1¼ cups all-purpose flour

1½ teaspoons paprika or smoked paprika

4 or 5 medium green tomatoes, cored and sliced a scant ¼ inch thick

1   Prepare the pie dough as instructed, but divide it into three equal pieces. Shape each piece into a ball, flatten each ball into a ½-inch-thick disk, and wrap the balls individually in plastic wrap. Refrigerate for at least 1½ hours.

2   To make the pimento cheese, combine the cheddar cheeses, mayonnaise, cream cheese, Worcestershire sauce, cayenne, ¼ teaspoon salt, and ⅛ teaspoon ground black pepper in a food processor. Pulse the mixture repeatedly, until well combined but not pureed. Add the pimentos and pulse again several times, until well combined but not too smooth. The mixture should have some texture and visible flecks of pimentos. Transfer to jars or crocks, cover, and refrigerate. Allow to sit in the refrigerator for at least a few hours, if possible, before using.

3   Next, make the galette filling. Heat the oil in a large skillet over medium heat and add the bacon. After a couple of minutes—when the bacon has rendered a bit of fat—add the onion. Continue to cook the bacon until it is good and crisp. Using a slotted spoon, transfer the bacon and onion to a plate and set it aside. Leave enough bacon fat in the skillet to coat it well.

4   Mix the flour and paprika on a plate and put it in your work area near the stove. Generously salt and pepper the tomato slices on both sides and put them nearby also.

5   Dredge both sides of each tomato slice in the flour mixture and place the slices in the skillet without crowding them. Fry for about 1 minute on each side, just long enough to soften them. Transfer the slices to a platter as they come out of the skillet. Preheat the oven to 375°F and get out three shallow 9-inch pie pans.

6   Working with one portion of dough at a time (and leaving the others in the refrigerator), roll it on a lightly floured surface into a circle 9½ inches in diameter. Fit the circle into the pie pan and transfer to the refrigerator. Repeat with the remaining two portions of dough.

7   Take the first pie shell out of the refrigerator. Smear ½ cup of the pimento cheese over the middle 6 inches of the circle (just the flat portion, not up the sides). Place one tomato slice in the center and then, working in a circle, make two more slightly overlapping rows of tomatoes to cover the cheese. Fold the uncovered edge of the pastry up over the outer row of tomatoes, then spoon about one-third of the bacon and onion mixture over the still-exposed tomatoes. Refrigerate while you repeat this procedure for the other two galettes.

8   Bake the galettes until golden brown and bubbly, about 35 minutes (see Recipe for Success). Transfer the pie pans to a cooling rack and cool for 15 to 30 minutes before slicing and serving.

Recipe for Success

The reason I use pie pans here, rather than a baking sheet, is that some of the oil from the mayonnaise will leak out of the pimento cheese. With a baking sheet, it will simply run out all over the place. But a pie pan will contain the oil, which can then reabsorb into the galette while it cools.

Assuming you have two oven racks, you can bake all three of these at one time. Just stagger their positions and move them around—side to side, and higher to lower—midway through the baking so they brown evenly.

You will need only about half of the pimento cheese for this recipe. But, as every southern cook knows, pimento cheese has lots of uses—serve it on crackers and celery sticks, stuff it into deviled eggs, make tea sandwiches with it, and more.

CREAMY RED POTATO & PARMESAN TART

As far back as I can recall, my favorite potato dish has been potatoes *dauphinoise*, a rich gratin with a touch of garlic and cheese. This tart is modeled after it. Serve it for brunch or a formal dinner, where loose potatoes might come across as a bit unruly. It also travels beautifully for a picnic—it's delicious at any temperature—or to one of those farm-to-table style meals that have become so popular these days. It's not at all difficult to assemble, but do try to cook the potatoes the day ahead because they'll be much easier to slice thinly. **Makes 6 to 8 servings**

1 recipe Tart Pastry (page 30), divided as instructed in step 1 and refrigerated

FILLING

2 pounds medium red-skinned potatoes

1¼ cups heavy cream

1 large or 2 small garlic cloves, minced

3 tablespoons unsalted butter

1 large onion, chopped

1¼ cups grated Parmesan cheese

1   If you haven't already, prepare the pastry, dividing it into two pieces, one equal to two-thirds of the dough and the other to one-third. You'll need the larger portion for this recipe. Shape the larger portion into a disk about ¾ inch thick; wrap well in plastic wrap and refrigerate for at least 1½ hours. (Shape the remaining portion into a disk also; wrap and refrigerate, if you're going to use it within a day or two—there will be enough to make a couple of pot pie tops or the shell for a 6- to 7-inch pie—or freeze the dough and use within 2 months.)

2   On a lightly floured sheet of wax paper, roll the dough into a circle 12 to 12½ inches in diameter. Invert the pastry over a 9-inch tart pan with a removable bottom (see Recipe for Success for alternative pan choices), center it, then peel off the paper. Gently tuck the pastry into the pan without stretching it or cutting it on the upper edge. When the pastry is tucked into place, use a paring knife or a rolling pin to trim the pastry flush with the top of the pan. Refrigerate the shell for at least 1 hour, then partially prebake and cool according to the directions on page 18.

3   Put the potatoes in a saucepan with enough water to cover by at least 1 inch. Salt the water and bring to a boil over high heat. Reduce the heat and boil gently until the potatoes are just tender at the center when pierced with a toothpick, 20 to 25 minutes. Using a slotted spoon, transfer the potatoes to a plate and allow to cool completely. Peel the potatoes, then cover and refrigerate them for at least an hour or two or, preferably, overnight.

4   When you're ready to assemble the tart, heat the cream and garlic—on the stove or in the microwave—until good and hot but not boiling. Remove from the heat and set aside.

Continued

5   Melt the butter in a medium-size skillet over medium heat. Add the onion, salt lightly, and sauté until lightly browned, about 10 minutes. Remove from the heat and set aside. Meanwhile, get the potatoes out of the refrigerator and slice them very thin, slightly more than ⅛ inch thick. Preheat the oven to 375°F.

6   To assemble the tart, spoon about one-quarter of the onions over the bottom of the shell, spreading them evenly. Sprinkle ¼ cup of the Parmesan cheese on top. Using about one-third of the potatoes, make a single, tightly packed layer of potato slices on top of the cheese. Stir the hot cream, then drizzle ⅓ cup over the potatoes. Sprinkle with salt and pepper to taste; don't skimp on the salt. Finish the layer with ⅓ cup Parmesan cheese.

7   Make another layer of potatoes, cream, salt and pepper, and Parmesan cheese. Finally, make a layer of potatoes, cream, and salt and pepper, then check the level of the cream. It should almost cover the potatoes. If you think you need a little more, drizzle it here and there; better to err on the side of too much, rather than too little. Spread the remaining onions on top of the last layer of potatoes, then top them with the last ⅓ cup of Parmesan cheese.

8   Put the pan on a 14-inch-long sheet of aluminum foil and press the foil up around the sides of the pan; this will hold in any butter that wants to ooze out and smoke up your kitchen. Bake on the center oven rack until the pastry and top of the tart are golden brown and the tart is bubbly, about 45 minutes. Transfer the tart to a cooling rack and cool for at least 10 minutes before serving.

Recipe for Success

You don't necessarily have to use a removable-bottom tart pan here; it just makes for a particularly fetching presentation. You can also use a ceramic tart pan or a flan ring.

This tart begs for the flavor of bacon if you're serving it for brunch, which you certainly should. In that case, omit the butter and crisp-fry 4 slices of bacon, setting the slices aside. Spoon off all but 2 to 3 tablespoons of the bacon fat, add the onion, and sauté as directed. Crumble the bacon over the top of the tart when you add the last layer of cheese. Bake as usual.

FREE-FORM ZUCCHINI & TOMATO TART

Boring old zucchini gets a makeover in this summery tart, with tomatoes underneath and a crunchy Parmesan and panko au gratin–style topping. **Makes 6 to 8 servings**

1 recipe Go-To Pie Dough (page 22) or Whole Wheat Pie Dough (page 26), refrigerated

FILLING

3 medium zucchini

3 tablespoons olive oil, plus more for drizzling on top

3 garlic cloves, minced

½ cup grated Parmesan cheese

⅓ cup panko bread crumbs

2 teaspoons dried basil

2 medium ripe tomatoes, cored and very thinly sliced

3 to 4 tablespoons heavy cream (optional, but nice)

1 If you haven't already, prepare the pastry and refrigerate it for at least 1½ hours.

2 Cut the zucchini on the bias into slices nearly ¼ inch thick. Heat the 3 tablespoons olive oil in a large skillet over medium heat. Add the zucchini slices and salt and pepper them liberally. Sauté for 2 minutes, stirring often. Add the garlic and sauté for another minute. Remove from the heat and transfer the zucchini and garlic to a platter.

3 Combine the Parmesan cheese, panko, and basil in a small bowl. Set aside. Preheat the oven to 375°F.

4 On a floured surface, roll the pastry into a circle about 13 inches in diameter, or into a large oblong, in either case about ⅛ inch thick. Transfer to a large rimmed baking sheet. (The easiest way to do this is to roll it directly on a large sheet of parchment paper, then lift the parchment right onto the sheet.) Sprinkle 3 to 4 tablespoons of the Parmesan mixture over the surface of the dough, leaving a 1½-inch uncovered border around the perimeter.

5 Arrange a layer of tomato slices over the Parmesan mixture on the pastry, again leaving the border uncovered. It's fine to partially overlap the slices. Sprinkle 1 tablespoon of the remaining Parmesan mixture over the tomatoes. Now arrange slightly overlapping rows of zucchini slices over the tomatoes. Lightly salt and pepper the slices when they're all in place. Fold the uncovered edge of the pastry up over the edge of the filling. If you're using it, drizzle the cream over the surface of the zucchini.

6 Bake the tart on the center oven rack for 30 minutes. Slide the tart out, sprinkle with the remaining Parmesan mixture, then drizzle several tablespoons of olive oil over the top to moisten the topping. Bake until the top of the tart is a rich golden brown, 10 to 15 minutes more. Serve hot.

Recipe for Success

I specify two dough possibilities, but virtually any single crust pastry recipe in this collection will work just fine here.

Keep in mind that you're not trying to fully cook the zucchini slices on the stovetop, just soften them up a little, make them flexible, and infuse them with garlic flavor; they'll finish cooking in the oven. We get the slices out of the pan right away so the residual heat doesn't continue to cook them.

SAVORY WINTER VEGETABLE CRISP

Here's a delightful dinner pie, especially for those who shy away from making pie pastry. Instead of a pie dough, you make a crumb crust from crackers and panko bread crumbs—no more difficult than making a graham cracker crust. About half the crumbs are pressed into your pie pan and prebaked, again like a graham cracker crust, and the rest is sprinkled over the top. What goes between the layers is a delicious medley of winter vegetables moistened with a touch of broth and a dab of cream. It's really good, and quite adaptable to the larder. **Makes 6 servings**

CRUMB CRUST

1 cup finely crushed Ritz crackers or other "buttery" crackers

1 cup panko bread crumbs

½ cup grated Parmesan cheese

2 tablespoons all-purpose flour

8 tablespoons (1 stick) unsalted butter, melted

FILLING

2 tablespoons olive oil

½ large onion, chopped

1½ cups halved (or quartered, if large) Brussels sprouts

3 medium carrots, peeled and thinly sliced

1 cup peeled and diced (½-inch) red-skinned potatoes

1 cup sliced white mushroom caps

½ cup chicken broth or vegetable broth

⅓ cup heavy cream

1   Preheat the oven to 350°F. Butter a 9- or 9½-inch deep-dish pie pan and set it aside.

2   Combine the cracker crumbs, panko, Parmesan cheese, flour, and ¼ teaspoon each salt and ground black pepper in a large mixing bowl. Mix well. Add the melted butter and mix thoroughly, first with a fork or spoon and then with your fingers, to get it as evenly mixed as possible. Press half of the mixture into the bottom and very slightly up the sides of the pie pan. Bake on the center oven rack until light golden, 10 to 12 minutes. Transfer to a rack to cool. Turn the oven up to 375°F.

3   Heat the olive oil in a large skillet over medium heat. Add the onion and sauté for 5 minutes. Add the rest of the vegetables and the broth. Increase the heat a bit and cook, stirring occasionally, for 4 to 5 minutes. When you're not stirring, cover the pan intermittently so the veggies steam a bit and the moisture is retained. Your goal here is to end up with partially cooked veggies that still have a bit of crunch, so, as they reach that point, remove the pan from the heat and uncover it. Cool for about 15 minutes, stirring the veggies from time to time. If they need a little salt and pepper, add it now.

4   Spoon the veggies, and any broth in the skillet, over the crust. Drizzle the cream over the vegetables. Cover with aluminum foil and bake on the center oven rack for 25 minutes. Slide the pie pan out, uncover, and scatter the remaining half of the crumb mixture over the top. Reduce the heat to 350°F and bake until the top is golden brown and all the veggies are tender, about 15 minutes more. If the top starts to get too brown, cover with foil again. Transfer to a rack and cool for at least 10 minutes before serving.

Recipe for Success

If you want to make a slightly richer version of this dish, sprinkle a little melting cheese like cheddar, Gouda, or fontina—cut into small dice—over the veggies just before you add the crumb topping. Even crumbled feta would work nicely.

KALE, POTATO & RICOTTA CHEESE GALETTE

Kale has been the darling of the vegetable circuit for the past few years, and this free-form tart will only enhance its reputation. The braised kale is spread over small roasted potatoes and ricotta cheese, and finished with a dusting of Parmesan. It's a veggie lover's nirvana. Six slices will give you nice dinner-size portions, perhaps with a side dish like sliced cucumbers vinaigrette. Or cut the tart into smaller slices and serve it as an appetizer. **Makes 6 to 8 servings**

1 recipe Go-To Pie Dough (page 22), refrigerated

FILLING

2½ to 3 cups small fingerling or creamer potatoes

3 tablespoons olive oil, plus more for drizzling

1½ teaspoons chopped fresh rosemary

1 large onion, chopped

6 to 8 Tuscan kale leaves, stemmed and coarsely chopped

½ cup chicken broth

1¼ cups ricotta cheese

½ cup chopped kalamata or other full-flavored olives

½ cup grated Parmesan cheese

1   If you haven't already, prepare the pastry and refrigerate it for at least 1½ to 2 hours.

2   Preheat the oven to 400°F. Halve the potatoes—lengthwise if they're more oblong than round—and place them in a bowl. Drizzle with a little olive oil, then sprinkle with a little salt and 1 teaspoon of the rosemary. Arrange the potatoes on a large baking sheet—preferably lined with parchment—and bake until tender, about 20 minutes. Transfer the sheet to a cooling rack. Leave the oven on.

3   Heat the 3 tablespoons olive oil in a large skillet over medium heat and add the onion. Sauté for 5 minutes, then stir in the kale and chicken broth. When the kale starts to wilt, cover the pan and gently braise the kale until tender, about 10 minutes. Uncover the pan and continue to cook until most of the liquid has evaporated. Set aside to cool.

4   In a small bowl, mix the ricotta cheese, olives, and the remaining ½ teaspoon rosemary with salt and pepper to taste. Set aside.

5   Lightly flour a large sheet of parchment paper and place the dough in the center. Roll the dough into a squared-off oblong about 16 inches long by 14 inches wide. Lift the paper and pastry onto a large baking sheet. (Or, you can roll the dough directly on your floured work surface, then transfer the rolled pastry to the baking sheet by hand.)

6   Leaving a 1½- to 1¾-inch border all around, scatter the potatoes here and there over the pastry. Dollop the cheese mixture all around it. Cover the potatoes and cheese with the braised kale. Fold the dough border up and over the filling to contain it; the dough will form pleats as you do so.

7   Bake the galette on the center oven rack for 35 minutes, then slide the tart out and sprinkle the Parmesan cheese evenly over the top. Drizzle a little olive oil on top. Slide the tart back into the oven and bake for 5 minutes more. Transfer the sheet to a cooling rack and cool for at least 10 to 15 minutes before serving.

Recipe for Success

You have some options here, cheese-wise and greens-wise. You can stir a few tablespoons grated Parmesan or Romano cheese into the ricotta to punch up the flavor, if you like. You could also add some diced sun-dried tomatoes. For the greens, spinach or Swiss chard would also do nicely, though since both lose even more of their volume than kale does, I'd increase their quantity by as much as 50 percent.

I like to braise greens—and plenty of other veggies, for that matter—in chicken broth. But this can easily become a meatless dish by using vegetable broth instead.

SWEET POTATO & HERB PARMESAN GALETTES

This recipe makes a threesome of the prettiest, tastiest little sweet potato tarts you've ever encountered—high praise from a fellow who usually finds sweet potatoes kind of boring. The potatoes' royal treatment includes a quick flash in the pan with chopped onion to soften up the slices. Then they're layered in the tart, dusted with sage-and-oregano'd Parmesan cheese, and finally drizzled with cream before being baked to golden perfection; think sweet potatoes au gratin, on a crust. It's enough to turn the most indifferent sweet potato eater into a rabid fan. **Makes 6 servings**

1 recipe Go-To Pie Dough (page 22), divided as instructed in step 1 and refrigerated

FILLING

3 tablespoons olive oil

½ large onion, finely chopped

3 sweet potatoes, peeled and sliced about ⅛ inch thick

1 to 1¼ cups grated Parmesan cheese

1½ teaspoons crumbled dried sage

1½ teaspoons dried oregano

¾ cup heavy cream

1   Prepare the pie dough as directed, but divide it into three equal pieces. Shape into balls, then flatten the balls into disks about ½ inch thick on a lightly floured surface. Wrap individually in plastic wrap, then refrigerate for 1½ hours.

2   Heat the olive oil in a large skillet, preferably nonstick, over medium heat. Add the onion and sauté for 3 to 4 minutes. Add the sweet potatoes. Salt and pepper to taste, then cook the potatoes, stirring often, for about 3 minutes. You're just trying to soften the slices and make them slightly flexible, not fully cook them. Immediately scrape the contents of the pan onto a platter and set aside to cool. Mix the Parmesan, sage, and oregano in a small bowl and place in your work area. Preheat the oven to 375°F.

3   Working with one piece of dough at a time and keeping the other two pieces of dough in the refrigerator, roll the dough on a floured work surface into a circle 8 or 8½ inches in diameter. Transfer to a large baking sheet, leaving enough room for a second circle of dough. (You can also do the rolling and assembly directly on parchment paper, then lift the parchment and galettes onto the baking sheet.)

4   Leaving a ¾-inch border all around, sprinkle about 2 tablespoons of the Parmesan mixture over the surface of the dough. Cover the cheese with 4 or 5 overlapping layers of sweet potato slices and sautéed onion. Sprinkle the top with another 2 tablespoons of the cheese mixture. Fold the uncovered border of the pastry up over the potato slices. Slowly drizzle 3 to 4 tablespoons cream over the potatoes.

5   Repeat for the next galette. Refrigerate the first two galettes on the baking sheet while you make the last one in a pie pan or on other smaller sheet. (You may end up with leftover sweet potato slices. Use them in soups, stews, or sautés.)

6   Bake the galettes until golden brown and bubbly, about 35 minutes. Midway though the baking, change the positions of the pans so the galettes bake evenly. Transfer the galettes to a rack. Cool for 10 to 15 minutes before serving.

Recipe for Success

Nothing says that you can't make two medium-size galettes—or even one big one—out of this recipe. Each way has its advantages. Simply divide the dough and the other ingredients accordingly, and roll the dough no more than ⅛ inch thick.

CREAM OF COLLARDS TARTE AU GRATIN

Collards are just about my favorite vegetable on earth, right up there with kale and Swiss chard, and I use them as frequently as I can in my dinner pies. Often they'll take on a supporting role, but in this tart they're the main attraction and gussied up in a way you seldom see this "lowbrow" vegetable prepared. The creamy richness of this tart is perfect with grilled or roasted meats. **Makes 8 to 10 servings**

1 recipe Go-To Pie Dough (page 22), refrigerated

FILLING

1 good-size bunch fresh collards

3 slices bacon

½ large onion, chopped

1½ cups chicken broth or vegetable broth

½ large baking potato, peeled

1 cup heavy cream

½ cup grated Parmesan cheese

½ cup panko bread crumbs

2 tablespoons unsalted butter, melted

1   If you haven't already, prepare the pastry and refrigerate it for at least 1½ hours.

2   On a lightly floured sheet of wax paper, roll the dough into a 13- to 13½-inch circle. Invert the pastry over a 9½- to 10-inch tart pan, center it, then peel off the paper. Gently tuck the pastry into the pan without stretching it, and sculpt the edge into an upstanding ridge. Refrigerate the shell for 1 hour, then partially prebake and cool according to the directions on page 18.

3   Cut and discard the center stems from the collards. Stack the leaves and cut them crosswise into ¼- to ½-inch-wide strips. Put these strips in a tub of water and agitate well to clean them. Transfer to a colander and drain well. Set aside. (You should have about 8 cups packed collards.)

4   In a very large skillet or stovetop casserole, cook the bacon over medium heat until crisp. Transfer the bacon to a plate to cool. Add the onion to the bacon fat and sauté, stirring often, for 7 to 8 minutes. Add the collards. Sauté for 5 minutes, turning the greens frequently with tongs to help cook them evenly. Add the broth.

5   Using the large holes of a box grater, grate the potato and immediately add the gratings to the pan. (You should have about ¾ cup grated potato.) Add a scant ½ teaspoon salt. Stir, and bring the liquid to a simmer. Cover and gently braise the collards until tender, about 15 minutes. By the time the collards are done, there should be just a little liquid glaze left in the pan. Regulate this by removing the lid during the last few minutes, if you have too much liquid, or by adding a little more broth or water, as needed. Pepper the greens to taste.

6   Stir the cream into the greens and bring to a low boil. Gently boil the greens for 2 to 3 minutes to thicken them up a bit. Remove from the heat and stir in the Parmesan cheese. Taste, and add more salt if you like. Set aside to cool a bit while you preheat the oven to 350°F.

7   Crumble the bacon into the tart shell. Add the collard mixture, spreading the greens evenly. Bake on the center oven rack for 30 minutes. Slide the rack out and carefully spread the panko crumbs evenly over the collards. Drizzle the melted butter over the crumbs. Bake the tart until the crumbs are golden brown, about 15 minutes more. Transfer the tart to a rack and cool for 20 to 30 minutes before slicing. The tart will become denser as it cools.

Recipe for Success

To keep this tarte au gratin as pure as possible, I don't add flour or any other powdered starch to the dish. Instead, we rely on the starch in the potato to help thicken things up—that's the primary reason for its appearance here. Grating the potato helps release quite a bit of the available starch and allows the potato to more or less disappear into the dish.

CURRIED WINTER SQUASH GALETTE WITH ONION & APPLE

When you write cookbooks, people often ask you how you come up with all of your recipe ideas. I like to say that I can find inspiration just about anywhere—from a photo, in my reading, during a casual conversation, or in my travels. Sometimes, inspiration for a new dish is borrowed from an "old" dish, in this case a warming curried winter squash and apple soup that I like to make in the fall and winter. Like the soup, this galette takes advantage of winter squash's uncommon affinity for curry seasoning. The diced apple adds a sweet note, but the caramelized onions, curry, and Brie leave no doubt that this is a savory tart first, and one that would go beautifully with a salad of greens, toasted pecans, blue cheese, and vinaigrette. **Makes 8 to 10 servings**

1 recipe Yeasted Butter Pastry
  (page 31), refrigerated

FILLING

3 tablespoons unsalted butter

5 cups halved and thinly sliced
  sweet onions

2 cups peeled, diced (½-inch)
  winter squash

2 teaspoons curry powder

1 cup peeled, diced (½-inch)
  Granny Smith or other firm tart
  apple

2 tablespoons light brown sugar

2 tablespoons apple cider vinegar

4 to 5 ounces Brie cheese, cut into
  small chunks

1   If you haven't already, prepare the pastry as instructed, moving it to the refrigerator for the second half of the rising.

2   Melt the butter in a large stovetop casserole over medium-low heat. Add the onions; salt and pepper them lightly. Cover and cook, stirring occasionally, for 10 minutes. Remove the lid, raise the heat to medium, and continue to cook for 5 minutes more.

3   Add the squash and curry powder to the onions. Sauté for 1 minute, then add the apple and 2 to 3 tablespoons water. Cover and cook for 5 minutes, then uncover and continue to cook until most of the "loose" liquid has cooked off but it is still a little saucy. Stir in the brown sugar and vinegar and cook for another minute or so. Remove from the heat and transfer the filling to a platter. Set aside and cool to room temperature while you preheat the oven to 375°F.

4   Get out a large rimless baking sheet. On a large sheet of parchment paper, roll the dough into an oblong about 14 inches long and 12 inches wide. Lift the paper onto your baking sheet and trim the paper to fit. (Lacking parchment paper, you can roll the dough on your floured work surface and simply lift it onto your lightly buttered baking sheet.)

5   Spread the cooled filling evenly over the dough, leaving a 1½-inch uncovered border all the way around. Fold the dough border up and over the filling to contain it; the dough will form pleats as you do so.

6   Bake the galette on the center oven rack until the edge is golden brown, about 35 minutes. Slide out the oven rack and carefully place the chunks of Brie here and there over the filling. Slide the galette back in and bake just until the cheese is soft and melty, about 5 minutes more. Transfer the pan to a cooling rack and cool for 5 minutes, then slide the galette directly onto the rack and cool for 5 more minutes before serving.

Recipe for Success

Once you've added the squash to your pan, the trick is to cook it until it's done, but not soft and mushy. As soon as it reaches the point that it's barely tender when you pierce it with a toothpick, remove it from the heat.

   If you find the dough hard to handle when you're folding the border over the filling, use a dough scraper or spatula to help lift it. Or, you can simply lift up the parchment paper itself to coax the edge of the pastry over the filling.

FREE-FORM FRENCH ONION TART

This delicious tart borrows flavor and form from a couple of dishes I've always loved: French onion soup topped with melty cheese, and *pissaladière*, the onion pizza that's a specialty of Nice in southern France. Whereas the latter is built on a yeasted bread dough, our version is made with a flaky pastry. This is rich and flavorful enough to be served in small wedges, as a small-plate appetizer. But it's equally wonderful as a main dish, accompanied by a large and colorful garden salad. **Makes 6 to 10 servings**

1 recipe Go-To Pie Dough (page 22), refrigerated

FILLING

4 tablespoons (½ stick) unsalted butter

3 large sweet onions, preferably Vidalias, halved and thinly sliced (about 7 cups)

¾ cup beef broth

1 tablespoon dry sherry or Cognac (optional)

¾ cup oil-cured black olives, pitted and sliced

1½ cups grated Swiss or Jarlsberg cheese

1 If you haven't already, prepare the pastry and refrigerate it for at least 1½ hours.

2 Melt the butter in a large skillet over medium heat. Add the onions, and salt and pepper them lightly. Sauté the onions until limp, 10 to 12 minutes.

3 Start adding the beef broth, about ¼ cup at a time. Continue cooking the onions, stirring occasionally, 12 to 15 minutes longer, adding more broth as it evaporates. You don't want the liquid to evaporate too quickly, so cover the skillet periodically to keep the onions moist. If you're adding it, stir in the sherry or Cognac during the last few minutes of cooking. When the onions are very soft, golden, and still a little thick-saucy, remove them from the heat. Taste, adding more salt and pepper if needed. Cool.

4 Preheat the oven to 375°F. On a lightly floured sheet of parchment, roll the dough into a circle about 12 inches in diameter. Slide the paper and dough onto a large rimless baking sheet.

5 Scrape the onions into the center of the pastry and spread them evenly, leaving a 1½-inch border around the edges. Using the paper to help you lift the dough—or by sliding a dough scraper under the pastry—fold the edge of the pastry over the onions; the dough will sort of pleat itself as you do so.

6 Bake on the center oven rack for 35 minutes. Slide the tart out, scatter the olives over the onions, then sprinkle on the cheese. Continue to bake just long enough to melt the cheese, 5 to 6 minutes more. Don't allow the cheese to bubble and blister or it won't stay soft.

7 Transfer the baking sheet to a cooling rack. Allow to cool for 5 minutes, then slide the paper and tart off the pan and onto the rack. Cool for another 5 to 10 minutes before serving.

Recipe for Success

A key step here is the cooking of the onions. Cooking them slowly brings out their sweetness and flavor. You'll probably have to put the lid on and take it off a few times in order to control the amount of moisture in the pan. You want just enough to keep the onions from scorching.

COLCANNON PIE

If you're a fan of colcannon—that hearty Irish dish of creamy mashed potatoes mixed with cooked greens—you'll love this pie. Of course, some might say that piling the goods into a buttery pastry is stretching the point, but they would, of course, be mistaken: The pastry transforms what we would typically consider a side dish into a main dish to be reckoned with. (A little leftover sauced beef or chicken on the side is perfect.) This recipe is written around braised cabbage, sandwiched between layers of mashed potatoes, but it's equally good made with fresh kale; see Recipe for Success. **Makes 6 to 8 servings**

1 recipe Go-To Pie Dough (page 22), refrigerated

FILLING

1 to 2 tablespoons vegetable oil

4 slices bacon, cut into ½-inch pieces

1 cup finely chopped onion

8 cups thinly sliced green cabbage

1 cup chicken broth

2 large baking potatoes (1½ to 1¾ pounds total), peeled and cut into chunks

½ cup whole milk

¼ cup sour cream

4 tablespoons (½ stick) unsalted butter, cut into several pieces

1½ cups grated sharp or extra-sharp cheddar cheese

1   If you haven't already, prepare the pastry and refrigerate it for at least 1½ hours.

2   On a lightly floured sheet of wax paper, roll the dough into a circle 13 to 13½ inches in diameter. Invert the pastry over a 9½-inch deep-dish pie pan, center it, then peel off the paper. Gently tuck the pastry into the pan without stretching it, then sculpt the edge into an upstanding ridge. Flute the ridge, if desired. Refrigerate the shell for at least 1 hour, then partially prebake and cool according to the directions on page 18. Preheat the oven to 350°F.

3   Heat the oil in a very large skillet over medium heat. Add the bacon and cook until much of the fat is rendered and the bacon is starting to crisp. Stir in the onion, sauté for 2 to 3 minutes, and then add the cabbage. (If your skillet isn't quite large enough to hold all of it, add half of the cabbage first, then cook it down a bit before adding the rest.) Lightly salt and pepper to taste.

4   When all of the cabbage has started to wilt, add ½ cup of the chicken broth. Cover and braise the cabbage for 7 to 10 minutes. Add the remaining ½ cup broth, then cover the skillet again and continue to cook until the cabbage is good and tender, about 10 minutes more. You want the cabbage to be damp, but not overly wet. Uncover for the last few minutes if you need to boil off some liquid. Set aside.

5   Put the potatoes in a large saucepan with plenty of salted water to cover. Bring to a boil over high heat, reduce the heat, and boil gently until the potatoes are tender, about 10 minutes. Drain, reserving the liquid.

6   Put the milk, sour cream, and butter in the still-hot saucepan. Let them warm for a minute, then return the drained potatoes to the pan. Mash well with a hand masher, adding a little of the potato water if needed; the ideal texture is neither too loose nor too firm, but right in the middle. (Use the rest of the potato water for soup stock, if you like.) Mix in salt and pepper to taste, then stir in 1 cup of the cheddar cheese.

7   To assemble the pie, spread about one-third of the mashed potatoes evenly in the pie shell. Pile the cabbage on top, spreading it around. Top with the remaining mashed potatoes. Sprinkle the remaining ½ cup cheese on top. Bake on the center oven rack for 30 minutes. Since everything is already cooked, there will be few visual clues of significance. You're simply baking the crust to golden perfection.

Recipe for Success

Kale is often used in place of cabbage in the traditional version of colcannon. It can be used here, as well, with some adjustments. First, unlike cabbage, fresh kale should be meticulously washed. Agitate the leaves in plenty of water to remove grit and dirt. Tear the leaves from the stems and chop well, discarding the stems. (You'll need 8 cups tightly packed leaves.) Sauté the onion and bacon as instructed, but you'll need more broth to steam-cook the kale until it is tender. Add 2 cups broth and simmer the kale—tightly covered—until it is tender, 20 to 30 minutes. Keep at least ¼ inch of broth in the pan at all times. When the kale is done, lift it out with tongs and save the liquid in the pan for soup stock. Proceed with the assembly, using the kale as you would the cabbage.

If you're looking for a slightly fancier presentation, use a 10-inch tart pan instead of a deep-dish pie pan.

LOADED BAKED POTATO TART

Secretly, at least, I think everyone loves a baked stuffed potato. There's probably no better vehicle for sour cream, chives, bacon bits, and cheese than a baked potato. But there's another way to give the basic idea a new set of wings—namely, this tart. Instead of big spuds, we use small fingerling or creamer potatoes and roast them with a bit of olive oil and salt. We layer these in our tart shell with sautéed onions and bacon bits, and top with a mustardy sour cream custard seasoned with chives. All the usual suspects are here; they're just playing slightly different roles, and I think you'll be very happy with the production. **Makes 8 servings**

1 recipe Go-To Pie Dough (page 22), refrigerated

FILLING

12 ounces small fingerling or creamer potatoes

1 to 2 tablespoons olive oil

2 tablespoons unsalted butter

1 large onion, halved and thinly sliced

6 to 8 slices bacon

4 large eggs

¾ cup half-and-half

½ cup heavy cream

½ cup sour cream

1½ tablespoons all-purpose flour

3 tablespoons chopped fresh chives

1 tablespoon Dijon mustard

2 cups grated sharp cheddar cheese

1   If you haven't already, prepare the pastry and refrigerate it for at least 1½ to 2 hours.

2   On a lightly floured sheet of wax paper, roll the dough into a 13- to 13½-inch circle. Invert the pastry over a 9½- to 10-inch tart pan, center it, then peel off the paper. Gently tuck the pastry into the pan without stretching it, and sculpt the edge into an upstanding ridge. Refrigerate the shell for 1 hour, then partially prebake and cool according to the directions on page 18. Preheat the oven to 400°F.

3   Halve the potatoes—lengthwise if they're more oblong than round—and place them in a mixing bowl. Add the olive oil and salt to taste; toss well to coat. Transfer the potatoes to a large baking sheet, preferably one lined with parchment, and roast the potatoes just until tender, about 20 minutes. Transfer the baking sheet to a rack to cool. Turn the oven down to 375°F.

4   Melt the butter in a large skillet over medium heat and add the onion. Sauté, stirring often, until golden brown, 12 to 15 minutes. Use a slotted spoon to transfer the onions to a plate. Add the bacon to the skillet and cook until crisp. Transfer the bacon to another plate to cool.

5   Whisk the eggs in a large bowl. Whisk in the half-and-half, heavy cream, and sour cream. Whisk in the flour, chives, mustard, ¾ teaspoon salt, and ¼ teaspoon ground black pepper.

6   Arrange the roasted potatoes and sautéed onions in your tart shell. Top with 1 cup of the cheddar cheese. Crumble half of the bacon over the cheese. Whisk the custard again, then slowly pour it over everything. Top with the remaining 1 cup cheese and the remaining bacon, crumbled.

7   Bake the tart on the center oven rack until golden brown and slightly puffy, 40 to 45 minutes. Transfer to a rack and cool for at least 30 minutes before serving.

Recipe for Success

For a nice touch, I like to add a couple of minced garlic cloves to the potatoes when they roast. I end up with little bits of dark-roasted garlic on the baking sheet, which I add right to the filling.

QUICHES & THEIR COUSINS

ARTICHOKE HEART, OLIVE & SUN-DRIED TOMATO QUICHE

Sometimes it's nice (i.e., convenient) to build a quiche around a few pantry items and with a minimum of stovetop prep—that's what this quiche is all about. The primary ingredients are a familiar trio we're more accustomed to seeing on an antipasto platter, but their compatibility really shines through here. Add a caramelized onion and some Parmesan cheese, and you have one fine quiche. **Makes 8 servings**

1 recipe Go-To Pie Dough (page 22) or Whole Wheat Pie Dough (page 26), refrigerated

FILLING

2½ tablespoons unsalted butter

1 large onion, halved and thinly sliced

2 garlic cloves, minced

1½ cups drained and quartered canned artichoke hearts

½ cup pitted and coarsely chopped olives

½ cup chopped oil-packed sun-dried tomatoes

4 large eggs

1¼ cups half-and-half

¼ cup heavy cream

1 cup grated Parmesan cheese

1½ tablespoons all-purpose flour

1 tablespoon chopped fresh basil or 1 teaspoon dried basil

1   If you haven't already, prepare the pastry and refrigerate it for at least 1½ to 2 hours.

2   On a lightly floured sheet of wax paper, roll the dough into a 13- to 13½-inch circle. Invert the pastry over a 9½- to 10-inch tart pan, center it, then peel off the paper. Gently tuck the pastry into the pan without stretching it, and sculpt the edge into an upstanding ridge. Refrigerate the shell for 1 hour, then partially prebake and cool according to the directions on page 18. Preheat the oven to 375°F.

3   Melt the butter in a large skillet over medium heat. Add the onion and sauté until soft and light golden, 12 to 15 minutes. Stir in the garlic and cook for another minute. Remove from the heat and set aside to cool briefly.

4   Spread the onions evenly in the tart shell. Scatter the artichoke hearts, olives, and sun-dried tomatoes over them.

5   Whisk the eggs in a large mixing bowl. Whisk in the half-and-half, heavy cream, Parmesan cheese, flour, basil, ¾ teaspoon salt, and ground black pepper to taste. Carefully pour or ladle the custard into the shell.

6   Bake the quiche on the center oven rack until golden brown and puffy, 35 to 45 minutes. Transfer the quiche to a cooling rack and cool for at least 30 minutes before serving.

FRESH CORN, TOMATO & GREEN OLIVE QUICHE

This Tex-Mex quiche contains everything but the kitchen sink, so be sure to use a generously proportioned deep-dish pie pan. Given the amount of stuff in it, the filling is textured and coarse, not smooth and custardy like your typical quiche. A little bowl of chili or a side of guacamole would round out the menu nicely. **Makes 8 servings**

1 recipe Go-To Pie Dough (page 22) or Cornmeal Pie Dough (page 28), refrigerated

FILLING

3 tablespoons unsalted butter

1 medium onion, chopped

½ green bell pepper, chopped

1 cup fresh-cut corn kernels

1 cup halved cherry or grape tomatoes

2 garlic cloves, minced

1¼ teaspoons chili powder

¾ teaspoon ground cumin

½ teaspoon smoked paprika

4 large eggs

1 cup half-and-half or whole milk

½ cup heavy cream

2 tablespoons sour cream

1½ tablespoons all-purpose flour

½ cup halved green olives with pimentos or black olives

½ cup pickled jalapeño peppers, drained and chopped

2 cups grated pepper Jack or sharp cheddar cheese

1   If you haven't already, prepare the pastry and refrigerate it for at least 1½ to 2 hours.

2   On a lightly floured sheet of wax paper, roll the dough into a 13- to 13½-inch circle. Invert the pastry over a 9½-inch deep-dish pie pan or a similar-size tart pan, center it, then peel off the paper. Gently tuck the pastry into the pan without stretching it, and sculpt the edge into an upstanding ridge. Refrigerate the shell for 1 hour, then partially prebake and cool according to the directions on page 18. Preheat the oven to 375°F.

3   Melt the butter in a large skillet over medium heat and stir in the onion and bell pepper. Sauté for 5 minutes, then stir in the corn kernels. Cover and continue to cook the mixture, stirring occasionally, until the corn is cooked but still a bit crunchy, about 5 minutes more. Stir in the tomatoes, garlic, chili powder, cumin, and smoked paprika. Salt lightly. Cook, uncovered, for 2 minutes more, stirring often so the spices don't scorch. Remove from the heat and allow to cool.

4   Whisk the eggs in a large mixing bowl until blended. Add the half-and-half, heavy cream, sour cream, flour, ¾ teaspoon salt, and ground black pepper to taste. Whisk well and set aside.

Continued

5 Spread the cooked vegetables evenly in the pie shell. Scatter the olives, jalapeños, and 1½ cups of the cheese over them. Briefly whisk the custard again, then pour it slowly into the shell. Top with the remaining ½ cup cheese.

6 Bake on the center oven rack until the quiche is puffed and golden brown on top and there's no evidence of uncooked egg in the middle, 40 to 45 minutes. Transfer the quiche to a rack and cool for at least 1 hour before serving.

Recipe for Success

This quiche would also be good with a little seasoned ground beef in it. Just cut back a little bit on each of the solids and substitute about 8 ounces ground beef. Brown it with the sautéed mixture and spread it in the shell.

Sure, you can use frozen corn kernels here. Let them thaw on paper towels, then add to the skillet.

FRESH CORN PUDDING PIE

We go a little crazy when fresh corn season rolls around and every farm stand we pass is stacked to the rafters with sweet, plump ears. We usually blanch, cut, and freeze a bushel or more. But there's still a handful of corn dishes that are nonnegotiable, ones that wouldn't be quite the same made with anything but sweet, fresh-cut kernels; this one is near the top of that list. As the name suggests, this is essentially a corn pudding. But because it has a cornmeal-thickened base, the texture is a little on the dense side. Layer on the flavor of extra-sharp cheddar cheese, and you've got a savory pie destined for summer greatness. Serve with sliced cukes and cherry tomatoes dressed with a basil vinaigrette. **Makes 8 servings**

1 recipe Go-To Pie Dough (page 22) or ½ recipe Cheddar Cheese Pastry (page 32), refrigerated

FILLING

1½ cups whole milk

3 tablespoons fine yellow cornmeal

4 tablespoons (½ stick) unsalted butter

2 teaspoons sugar

1 teaspoon Dijon mustard

1 cup finely chopped onion

2½ cups fresh-cut corn kernels (see Recipe for Success)

¾ cup small-curd cottage cheese

4 large eggs, lightly beaten

2 cups grated sharp or extra-sharp cheddar cheese

1 (4- to 5-ounce) can chopped green chiles, drained (optional)

1   If you haven't already, prepare the pastry and refrigerate it for at least 1½ to 2 hours.

2   On a lightly floured sheet of wax paper, roll the dough into a 13- to 13½-inch circle. Invert the pastry over a 9½-inch deep-dish pie pan, center it, then peel off the paper. Gently tuck the pastry into the pan without stretching it, and sculpt the edge into an upstanding ridge. Refrigerate the shell for 1 hour, then partially prebake and cool according to the directions on page 18. Preheat the oven to 350°F.

How to Shave an Ear

The secret to getting those kernels off the cob? A sharp chef's knife or large paring knife will do nicely, so long as it is sharp; dull knives tend to send the kernels and corn milk in all directions. Cut off the stem to create a flat surface the ear can rest on. Stand the corn, cut stem side down, on a cutting board. Steady the ear with your non-cutting hand. Then cut downward with your knife, using a sawing motion to remove the kernels.

There are also any number of handy devices for making quick work of the cutting process. One gizmo I like and can recommend is called the Corn Zipper, by Kuhn Rikon. You simply glide it along the ear and the razor-sharp blade slices the kernels right off.

Continued

3   Combine the milk and cornmeal in a small saucepan over medium heat. Gradually bring to a simmer, whisking constantly, until the mixture thickens to a cream-like consistency. Pour the mixture into a large bowl. Whisk in 2 tablespoons of the butter (cut into several pieces), the sugar, the mustard, 1 teaspoon salt, and ¼ teaspoon ground black pepper. Set aside.

4   Melt the remaining 2 tablespoons butter in a skillet over medium heat. Add the onion and corn and sauté until soft, 6 to 7 minutes.

5   Stir the corn sauté into the milk and cornmeal mixture. Whisk in the cottage cheese and eggs. Stir in the cheddar cheese and, if you like, the chiles.

6   Pour the filling into the partially prebaked shell. Bake on the center oven rack until the filling is set and no longer loose or soupy in the center, 40 to 45 minutes. When done, the sides will be slightly puffed up, and the middle a little less so. If the top of the pie hasn't browned and you'd like some browning, move the quiche to an upper rack in the oven for the last 10 minutes of baking. Transfer to a rack and cool for at least 30 minutes before slicing.

Recipe for Success

In spite of my little soapbox speech about using fresh corn for this wonderful pie, yes, you can use frozen corn. Let it thaw slightly, then add it to the skillet along with the onion.

Because you're using whole corn kernels, this filling has a rather coarse texture. For a smoother, more refined texture, combine the sautéed corn and cottage cheese in a food processor and pulse a few times to make a textured puree. Don't overdo it. Stir into the milk and cornmeal mixture, and proceed.

KALE & CRÈME FRAÎCHE QUICHE

I could be wrong about this, but I've been reading cookbooks for quite a few years now and I think the whole idea of adding crème fraîche to quiche is a relatively new one. It's not a bad idea; in fact, the crème fraîche gives the quiche a rich, custardy texture and a slight tanginess that's really something special. I think the richness benefits from a lean counterpart in the filling, and that's why I like adding kale. (I've tried it with both frozen and fresh—your choice.) A touch of Parmesan cheese and a flaky pastry crust, and you're in business. **Makes 8 servings**

1 recipe Whole Wheat Pie Dough (page 26), refrigerated

FILLING

3 tablespoons unsalted butter

½ large onion, chopped

2 garlic cloves, minced

2 to 3 cups coarsely chopped kale leaves (preferably Tuscan kale)

A little chicken broth or water

8 ounces crème fraîche

1 tablespoon all-purpose flour

¾ cup half-and-half

4 large eggs plus 1 egg yolk, lightly beaten

1 teaspoon Dijon mustard

Pinch of nutmeg

¼ cup grated Parmesan cheese

1 If you haven't already, prepare the pastry and refrigerate it for at least 1½ to 2 hours.

2 On a lightly floured sheet of wax paper, roll the dough into a 13- to 13½-inch circle. Invert the pastry over a 9½- to 10-inch tart pan, center it, then peel off the paper. Gently tuck the pastry into the pan without stretching it, and sculpt the edge into an upstanding ridge. Refrigerate the shell for 1 hour, then partially prebake and cool according to the directions on page 18. Preheat the oven to 375°F.

3 Melt the butter in a large skillet over medium heat, add the onion, and cook for 7 to 8 minutes. Stir in the garlic and kale and cook for 1 minute. Add just enough chicken broth or water to moisten everything, maybe ¼ to ⅓ cup. Salt lightly. Cover and steam-braise the kale until tender, 10 to 15 minutes, adding a little more water or broth as needed. Before you take the pan off the heat, remove the lid and cook off all of the excess moisture in the pan. Remove from the heat and set aside to cool.

4 Whisk the crème fraîche, flour, and about half of the half-and-half in a large bowl until smooth. Whisk in the lightly beaten eggs and yolk, ½ teaspoon salt, and plenty of ground black pepper. Finally, whisk in the mustard, nutmeg, and the remaining half-and-half.

5   Spread the onion and kale mixture evenly in the tart shell. Slowly pour or ladle the custard over the kale. Sprinkle the Parmesan cheese over the top. Bake the quiche on the center oven rack until puffed and golden brown on top, 35 to 40 minutes. Transfer to a rack and cool for at least 20 minutes before serving.

Recipe for Success

Crème fraîche is often compared to sour cream, which is sometimes recommended as a substitution. The two are similar: Both are made by adding friendly bacteria to cream. But sour cream has a lower fat content and a decidedly tangier flavor. Crème fraîche is richer, mellower, and sweeter. And unlike sour cream, crème fraîche won't curdle if it's heated. It's a little on the pricey side, but you can save quite a bit by making it at home. Just blend 2 tablespoons cultured buttermilk with 1 pint pasteurized whipping cream in a large jar. Cover the jar with cheesecloth secured by a rubber band. Let stand at room temperature for 12 to 24 hours to thicken. Stir, screw on the lid, and refrigerate. It will keep for at least 4 or 5 days.

SWISS CHARD & QUINOA QUICHE WITH A SESAME-STUDDED CRUST

I've been using a lot of quinoa for the last few years and I'm not sure which is increasing more quickly, the price of the stuff—*sheesh!*—or the number of ways I've come up with to use it. Unlike the silky-smooth consistency of many quiches, this one is more nubby and textured thanks to the quinoa and cottage cheese. And it's somewhat compact once it has cooled. Different, but still thoroughly enjoyable and delicious. The Swiss chard is delightful in the filling, but I've also used baby spinach and kale, so feel free to go renegade. Take note of how we do the seeded crust; it's a good little trick you can use on many of your dinner pies. **Makes 8 servings**

1 recipe Go-To Pie Dough (page 22), refrigerated

1 to 1½ tablespoons sesame seeds, toasted if you like

FILLING

2 tablespoons unsalted butter

½ large onion, chopped

2 garlic cloves, minced

1½ cups thinly sliced white mushroom caps

1 pound Swiss chard, stemmed and coarsely chopped (about 4 cups packed)

1 to 2 tablespoons water or chicken broth

3 large eggs

1¼ cups small-curd cottage cheese

½ cup grated Parmesan cheese

2 tablespoons pesto

1 to 1¼ cups cooked quinoa (see Recipe for Success)

1 If you haven't already, prepare the pastry and refrigerate it for at least 1½ to 2 hours.

2 On a lightly floured sheet of wax paper or parchment, roll the dough into a 10- to 11-inch circle. Sprinkle the dough evenly with the sesame seeds, then continue rolling—and embedding the seeds—until you have a 13- to 13½-inch circle. Invert the pastry over a 9½- to 10-inch tart pan so that the seeds are visible on the outside of the crust. Center the crust, then peel off the paper. Gently tuck the pastry into the pan without stretching it, and sculpt the edge into an upstanding ridge. Refrigerate the shell for 1 hour, then partially prebake and cool according to the directions on page 18. Preheat the oven to 375°F.

3 Melt the butter in a large skillet over medium heat. Add the onion and sauté for 5 to 6 minutes. Stir in the garlic and mushrooms. Cover and cook for several minutes more, long enough for the mushrooms to sweat considerably. Stir in the Swiss chard; salt everything lightly. Cover and steam the chard until well wilted, another 3 or 4 minutes; add a tablespoon or so of water or broth as it cooks if the pan seems to need it. Uncover the pan and continue to heat just long enough to cook off the excess moisture. Set aside.

4   Whisk the eggs in a large mixing bowl. Whisk in the cottage cheese, Parmesan cheese, pesto, ½ teaspoon salt, and ¼ teaspoon ground black pepper. Stir in the sautéed chard and cooked quinoa. Transfer the filling to the tart shell, smoothing the top with a spoon.

5   Bake the quiche on the center oven rack until puffy, golden brown, and set in the middle, 40 to 45 minutes. Transfer the quiche to a cooling rack and cool for at least 20 to 30 minutes before serving.

Recipe for Success

People often ask me what I do to my quinoa to make it taste so good. Let me preface my answer by saying that, much as I love the stuff, quinoa is pretty boring without doing something to it. The "something" in my case is usually to cook it in chicken broth with a healthy pinch of paprika and a pat of butter. Some might say that the butter nullifies the health benefits of eating quinoa in the first place, but I'll take my chances.

You should know that stirring pesto into your filling is going to give it a very slight St. Paddy's Day–like tinge. You'll scarcely notice it on the surface, because of the browning. But if you think that's a problem or will otherwise arouse suspicion at your dinner table—think picky child or finicky family member—substitute 2 teaspoons dried basil or 1 tablespoon chopped fresh basil.

RICOTTA, SPINACH & SAUSAGE QUICHE

Ricotta cheese makes a firm-textured quiche, with a filling that's a little drier and more sponge-like than your typical custard. If those adjectives sound less than appetizing, let me assure you that this is one delicious quiche. You're going to love it. **Makes 8 servings**

1 recipe Go-To Pie Dough (page 22), refrigerated

FILLING

3 tablespoons unsalted butter

1 large onion, chopped

2 garlic cloves, minced

12 ounces baby spinach, coarsely chopped

8 ounces fully cooked mild or hot Italian sausage, coarsely chopped

⅔ cup ricotta cheese

⅔ cup half-and-half or light cream

3 large eggs

1 teaspoon Dijon mustard

½ teaspoon dried basil

¾ cup grated Parmesan cheese

1 tablespoon all-purpose flour

1 If you haven't already, prepare the pastry and refrigerate it for at least 1½ to 2 hours.

2 On a lightly floured sheet of wax paper, roll the dough into a 13- to 13½-inch circle. Invert the pastry over a 9½-inch deep-dish pie pan or a similar-size tart pan, center it, then peel off the paper. Gently tuck the pastry into the pan without stretching it, and sculpt the edge into an upstanding ridge. Refrigerate the shell for 1 hour, then partially prebake and cool according to the directions on page 18. Preheat the oven to 350°F.

3 Melt the butter in a large skillet over medium heat. Add the onion and sauté until light golden, about 10 minutes. Stir in the garlic and spinach. Partially cover and cook until the spinach is wilted, 2 to 3 minutes. Remove from the heat, stir in the sausage, and set aside.

4 Combine the ricotta cheese, half-and-half, eggs, mustard, basil, ½ teaspoon salt, and ¼ teaspoon ground black pepper in a blender or food processor. Process briefly, just until smooth. Add ½ cup of the Parmesan cheese and the flour. Process again briefly.

5 Spread the spinach and sausage mixture evenly in the tart shell. Slowly pour the ricotta cheese custard over the mixture. Use a fork to gently nudge the solids so the custard settles. Sprinkle the remaining ¼ cup Parmesan cheese over the top.

6 Bake on the center oven rack until the filling is set and no longer loose or soupy in the center, 40 to 45 minutes. If the top needs a little browning, briefly run the quiche under the broiler. Transfer to a rack and cool for 10 to 15 minutes before serving.

Recipe for Success

Substitute cottage cheese for the ricotta, if you like. The filling will be a bit moister, but it's a good option if that's what you have on hand.

RICE & SPINACH TART

This tart is something of a cross between a savory rice pudding and a risotto, and a good indication of how much I enjoy both. I don't know about you, but I always seem to have leftover rice around. At some point I started adding it to my tarts and loved what a great filler it was: Not only was it a clever way to use up leftovers, but the rice added its own flavor to the filling. (For this reason, I encourage you to use a full-flavored rice, for instance one made with broth and wild rice, rather than plain white rice.) My wife, Bev, counts this on her short list of favorites in this collection. **Makes 8 to 10 servings**

1 recipe Go-To Pie Dough (page 22), refrigerated

FILLING

2 tablespoons unsalted butter

½ large onion, chopped

2½ to 3 cups sliced white mushroom caps

1 garlic clove, minced

¼ cup dry white wine

2 tablespoons olive oil or additional unsalted butter

12 ounces chopped spinach leaves or baby spinach

2 cups cooked rice

1 cup grated fontina or Gouda cheese

3 large eggs

1 cup whole milk

½ cup heavy cream

⅔ cup grated Parmesan cheese

1   If you haven't already, prepare the pastry and refrigerate it for at least 1½ to 2 hours.

2   On a lightly floured sheet of wax paper, roll the dough into a 13- to 13½-inch circle. Invert the pastry over a 9½- to 10-inch tart pan, center it, then peel off the paper. Gently tuck the pastry into the pan without stretching it, and sculpt the edge into an upstanding ridge. Refrigerate the shell for 1 hour, then partially prebake and cool according to the directions on page 18. Preheat the oven to 375°F.

3   Melt the butter in a large skillet over medium heat. Add the onion and sauté for 3 to 4 minutes. Stir in the mushrooms and garlic; salt lightly. Sauté until the mushrooms have softened, 2 to 3 minutes, then add the white wine. Increase the heat and continue to cook until most—but not quite all—of the liquid has evaporated. (You want a slight bit of glaze left in the pan. Lots of flavor there.) Scrape into a small bowl and set aside.

4   Put the skillet back over medium heat. Add the olive oil and stir in the spinach; salt lightly. Sauté until the spinach is wilted and soft, 2 to 3 minutes. Set aside.

5   To assemble the tart, fluff the rice with a fork so the grains are separate, then spread it evenly in the tart shell; don't compress it. Spoon the mushroom mixture and its juice evenly over the rice. Sprinkle the grated fontina over that, then spread the spinach around on top.

6   Whisk the eggs in a large bowl until evenly blended. Whisk in the milk, cream, Parmesan, ¾ teaspoon salt, and ¼ teaspoon ground black pepper. The cheese will make the custard look curdled, but it should be otherwise evenly blended. Slowly pour the custard over the filling.

7   Bake the tart on the center rack until slightly puffy and golden brown, 40 to 45 minutes. Transfer to a rack and cool for at least 15 minutes before serving.

Recipe for Success

I would often use 4 eggs in a tart of this size, but in this case I use just 3 since the rice itself acts as a binder and thickener, eliminating the need for another egg.

By design I do not use any herbs here. There's something special about the subtle flavor of the rice, mushrooms, spinach, and cheese, and they're best left to speak for themselves.

ROASTED ASPARAGUS & GOAT CHEESE QUICHE

This one's rich, roasted, and really, really good—the perfect end-of-winter, thank-God-it's-finally-spring quiche. Serve it with steamed and buttered creamer potatoes, with fresh strawberries for dessert. **Makes 8 servings**

1 recipe Go-To Pie Dough (page 22), refrigerated

FILLING

1 pound asparagus

Olive oil, for drizzling

2 garlic cloves, minced

2 tablespoons unsalted butter

1 large onion, chopped

4 to 6 ounces goat cheese

4 large eggs

½ cup whole milk

¼ cup sour cream

1 tablespoon all-purpose flour

1½ teaspoons Dijon mustard

1 teaspoon dried basil

1 cup heavy cream

1   If you haven't already, prepare the pastry and refrigerate it for at least 1½ to 2 hours.

2   On a lightly floured sheet of wax paper, roll the dough into a 13- to 13½-inch circle. Invert the pastry over a 9½- to 10-inch tart pan, center it, then peel off the paper. Gently tuck the pastry into the pan without stretching it, and sculpt the edge into an upstanding ridge. Refrigerate the shell for 1 hour, then partially prebake and cool according to the directions on page 18. Preheat the oven to 425°F.

3   Cut off and discard the woody bottom part of each asparagus spear—about the lower third—and put the usable sections in a large mixing bowl. Drizzle with 2 or 3 tablespoons olive oil; add the garlic and toss well to mix. Spread the asparagus out on a large rimmed baking sheet. Salt and pepper to taste, then bake-roast on the center oven rack just until tender, about 10 minutes for skinny spears and up to 15 minutes for fat ones. Transfer the sheet to a rack to cool. Turn the oven down to 375°F.

4   Meanwhile, melt the butter in a medium-size skillet over medium heat. Add the onion and sauté until light golden, about 10 minutes. Set aside to cool.

5 Spread the onions evenly in your tart shell. Put about half of the roasted asparagus spears on a chopping board and cut into approximate 1-inch pieces. Scatter these evenly over the onions. Crumble and scatter the goat cheese evenly over the asparagus. Arrange the remaining whole asparagus spears in some sort of decorative arrangement on top (see Recipe for Success).

6 Whisk the eggs in a large mixing bowl until blended. Add the milk, sour cream, flour, mustard, basil, ¾ teaspoon salt, and ground black pepper to taste and whisk until smooth. Whisk in the heavy cream. Slowly—so you don't displace the solids—pour or ladle the custard over everything in the tart shell. Bake on the center oven rack until the quiche is golden brown and puffy, about 45 minutes. Transfer to a rack and cool for at least 30 minutes before serving.

Recipe for Success

I think of this first as a spring tart, but I'll also prepare it when asparagus makes an unexpected appearance in the market—especially if it's on sale—at other times of year.

There will be a lot of good roasted garlic bits on the baking sheet after you roast the asparagus. Gather them up and drop them in the quiche before you bake it to accent the roasted flavor.

I'm not the artistic type, so I don't get as fancy with the top asparagus spears as I could. I'll just radiate them like the spokes of a bicycle wheel, or make two gently bowed rows of them, overlapping slightly in the middle. Feel free to go crazy and make it pretty.

QUICHE SCAMPI

Butter-sautéed shrimp and garlic is heavenly on pasta, but it's not half bad in a quiche, either, as you'll discover in this namesake dish. A handful of sliced cherry tomatoes and plenty of chopped parsley add color and flair, while the Parmesan cheese ties all the flavors together and gives the quiche an Italian accent we adore. This is best served the same day it's baked. **Makes 8 servings**

1 recipe Go-To Pie Dough (page 22), refrigerated

FILLING

3 tablespoons unsalted butter

8 to 12 ounces large shrimp, peeled and deveined

½ to ¾ cup halved cherry tomatoes or grape tomatoes

2 scallions, thinly sliced

4 or 5 garlic cloves, minced

3 tablespoons chopped fresh flat-leaf parsley

¼ teaspoon red pepper flakes

4 large eggs

1¼ cups half-and-half

¼ cup heavy cream

⅔ cup grated Parmesan cheese

1½ tablespoons all-purpose flour

1 teaspoon Dijon mustard

1   If you haven't already, prepare the pastry and refrigerate it for at least 1½ to 2 hours.

2   On a lightly floured sheet of wax paper, roll the dough into a 13- to 13½-inch circle. Invert the pastry over a 9½- to 10-inch tart pan, center it, then peel off the paper. Gently tuck the pastry into the pan without stretching it, and sculpt the edge into an upstanding ridge. Refrigerate the shell for 1 hour, then partially prebake and cool according to the directions on page 18. Preheat the oven to 375°F.

3   Melt the butter in a large skillet over medium heat. Add the shrimp and cook for 1 minute on the first side. Turn the shrimp over, then sprinkle the tomatoes, scallions, garlic, parsley, and red pepper flakes in the pan. Cook the shrimp for 2 minutes more, stirring occasionally (the shrimp will not be cooked through; they will finish cooking in the oven). Using a rubber spatula, scrape the contents of the skillet into your tart shell, spreading everything around as evenly as possible.

4   Whisk the eggs in a large bowl until evenly blended. Whisk in the half-and-half, heavy cream, Parmesan, flour, mustard, and ¾ teaspoon salt. Slowly—so you don't displace the solids—ladle the custard into your shell. Bake the quiche on the center oven rack for 25 minutes, then reduce the heat to 350°F and continue to bake until slightly puffy and golden brown on top, 10 to 15 minutes more. Transfer to a rack and cool for at least 30 minutes before serving.

Recipe for Success

Sometimes I'll trick myself into believing there's more shrimp in the quiche than there actually is by cutting each one into 2 or 3 smaller pieces once they've cooled off. Lots of smaller pieces just look like more shrimp than a few big ones do.

BACON, BLUE CHEESE & ROASTED TOMATO QUICHE

Of the many arguments I could make for roasting tomatoes as often as possible, this quiche is probably the most persuasive. The flavors are exquisite together, and the flaky whole wheat pastry adds a rustic touch and provides the perfect casing. It's just not the same without the roasted tomatoes. But if there's no chance you'll be roasting your own, many of the larger supermarkets now carry them in their salad bars, near the olives. In a pinch, you could substitute strips of roasted red pepper for the roasted tomatoes. **Makes 8 servings**

1 recipe Whole Wheat Pie Dough (page 26), refrigerated

FILLING

1 tablespoon olive oil or vegetable oil

2 slices bacon, cut in ¼-inch pieces

½ large onion, finely chopped

4 large eggs

1 cup half-and-half

½ cup heavy cream

1 teaspoon Dijon mustard

1 cup crumbled blue cheese

8 to 10 roasted tomatoes halves (see opposite)

¼ cup grated Parmesan cheese

1   If you haven't already, prepare the pastry and refrigerate it for at least 1½ to 2 hours.

2   On a lightly floured sheet of wax paper, roll the dough into a 13- to 13½-inch circle. Invert the pastry over a 9½- to 10-inch tart pan, center it, then peel off the paper. Gently tuck the pastry into the pan without stretching it, and sculpt the edge into an upstanding ridge. Refrigerate the shell for 1 hour, then partially prebake and cool according to the directions on page 18. Preheat the oven to 375°F.

3   Heat the oil in a medium-size skillet over medium heat. Stir in the bacon and onion; salt lightly. Cook, stirring, until the bacon is beginning to crisp, 5 to 6 minutes. Remove from the heat and set aside.

Roasting Tomatoes

I could live on nothing but roasted tomatoes. I eat them on toast—bruschetta!—toss them with cold pasta, add them to salads, put 'em on burgers. Here's how: Preheat your oven to 350°F. Start with 10 to 12 good-size ripe plum tomatoes. Core, halve lengthwise, and push out most of the seeds. Place the tomato halves, cut sides up, on a large rimmed baking sheet lined with parchment paper or oiled foil. Salt and pepper to taste, then drizzle liberally with olive oil and sprinkle with lots of minced garlic. Bake until soft, shrunken, and definitely done-looking, 1¼ to 1½ hours. Cool on the sheet for 15 minutes, then transfer to a covered glass container, covering them with a layer of olive oil. Store in the refrigerator for up to 8 weeks. They also freeze beautifully; just make a single flat layer in quart-size freezer bags and place in the freezer.

4   Whisk the eggs in a large bowl until evenly blended. Whisk in the half-and-half, heavy cream, mustard, ½ teaspoon salt, and ¼ teaspoon ground black pepper.

5   Sprinkle the blue cheese in the tart shell and spread it around evenly. Ladle on just enough custard to cover the cheese. Make a ring of tomato halves around the perimeter of the tart and place one in the center also. Scatter the sautéed onions and bacon over the tomatoes. Whisk the custard again, then slowly pour it over the tomatoes. Sprinkle the Parmesan cheese over the top.

6   Bake on the center oven rack for 30 minutes. Reduce the heat to 350°F and continue to bake until puffy and golden brown, 10 to 15 minutes more. Transfer to a cooling rack and cool for at least 30 minutes before serving.

Recipe for Success

Remember, you can always move your quiche up or down in the oven if it's browning too fast or not fast enough. I do this all the time. After 30 minutes, if the top is still pretty pale, I'll move the oven rack and quiche one position higher. A quiche without some nice browning on top lacks drama and doesn't make a good first taste impression.

Don't try to use fresh tomatoes here. No matter how good they are, the excess moisture will throw off the filling of this quiche.

SALMON, SMOKED CHEDDAR & DILL QUICHE

If you love smoked salmon, for brunch or any other time of day, prepare to make acquaintance with the quiche of your dreams. We begin by dolloping the shell with a smushed cream cheese, mustard, and dill mixture. Then we tuck lots of smoked salmon in between the dollops. Finally, all of it is covered with smoked cheddar and a rich, creamy custard. The layers of flavor meld into a smoked salmon nirvana. For brunch, serve home fries on the side and a little something sweet, like a fruit crisp, to cap off the meal. **Makes 8 servings**

1 recipe Go-To Pie Dough (page 22), refrigerated

FILLING

4 ounces cream cheese, at room temperature

½ cup finely chopped red onion

3 tablespoons chopped fresh dill

1 tablespoon Dijon mustard

6 ounces smoked salmon, flaked

1 to 1½ cups grated smoked cheddar cheese

4 large eggs

1 cup half-and-half

⅓ cup heavy cream

1 tablespoon all-purpose flour

1   If you haven't already, prepare the pastry and refrigerate it for at least 1½ to 2 hours.

2   On a lightly floured sheet of wax paper, roll the dough into a 13- to 13½-inch circle. Invert the pastry over a 9½- to 10-inch tart pan, center it, then peel off the paper. Gently tuck the pastry into the pan without stretching it, and sculpt the edge into an upstanding ridge. Refrigerate the shell for 1 hour, then partially prebake and cool according to the directions on page 18. Preheat the oven to 375°F.

3   Combine the cream cheese, red onion, dill, mustard, and plenty of black pepper in a small mixing bowl. Mash well with a large fork, then dollop the mixture here and there in the tart shell. Don't press it down or smooth it out. Scatter the flaked salmon around the cream cheese dollops. Sprinkle the cheddar cheese evenly over the top.

4   Whisk the eggs in a mixing bowl until frothy. Whisk in the half-and-half, heavy cream, flour, ½ teaspoon salt, and ground black pepper to taste. Slowly and evenly pour the custard over the solids.

5   Bake the tart on the center oven rack until the quiche has puffed a bit and the top is golden brown, about 40 minutes. Transfer to a rack and cool for at least 30 minutes before serving.

Recipe for Success

Smoked salmon is pricey, so for the sake of economy you don't need to include 6 ounces of it here. Fortunately, the flavor is bold and a little bit goes a long way.

GREEK CAULIFLOWER & SPINACH QUICHE

I love cauliflower, but it's admittedly bland and seldom, it seems, gets top billing in a quiche. But dress it up with some A-list players like feta cheese, spinach, garlic, and tomatoes, and you've got an ensemble cast that earns this quiche rave reviews every time. **Makes 8 servings**

1 recipe Go-To Pie Dough (page 22), refrigerated

FILLING

2½ tablespoons olive oil

1 large onion, halved and thinly sliced

2½ cups small cauliflower florets

½ cup chicken broth or water

2 cups packed chopped spinach leaves or baby spinach

2 plum tomatoes, cored and coarsely chopped

2 garlic cloves, minced

3 large eggs

⅔ cup heavy cream

⅔ cup half-and-half or light cream

2 tablespoons all-purpose flour

½ teaspoon Dijon mustard

½ teaspoon dried thyme

1 cup crumbled feta cheese

½ cup coarsely chopped black olives

½ cup grated Parmesan cheese (optional)

1   If you haven't already, prepare the pastry and refrigerate it for at least 1½ to 2 hours.

2   On a lightly floured sheet of wax paper, roll the dough into a 13- to 13½-inch circle. Invert the pastry over a 9½-inch deep-dish pie pan or a similar-size tart pan, center it, then peel off the paper. Gently tuck the pastry into the pan without stretching it, and sculpt the edge into an upstanding ridge. Refrigerate the shell for 1 hour, then partially prebake and cool according to the directions on page 18. Preheat the oven to 350°F.

3   Heat the olive oil in a large skillet over medium heat. Add the onion and sauté for 6 to 7 minutes. Stir in the cauliflower and sauté for 1 minute. Stir in the broth, spinach, tomatoes, and garlic. Salt lightly. Cook, stirring often, until the liquid evaporates and the cauliflower is just crisp-tender, 3 to 4 minutes. Remove from the heat and set aside.

Recipe for Success

One of the tricks here is to not overcook the cauliflower. I call this moment "crisp-tender," and it can be tricky to time it so the liquid has, simultaneously, evaporated. I'm being a little picky here, so don't sweat it too much; just do the best you can.

It almost goes without saying, but—with water instead of chicken broth—this makes a fine vegetarian main dish.

Continued

4   Whisk the eggs in a large bowl until frothy. Whisk in the heavy cream and half-and-half. Whisk in the flour, mustard, thyme, ½ teaspoon salt, and ground black pepper to taste.

5   Spoon the vegetables into the partially prebaked shell. Scatter the feta cheese and olives on top. Slowly pour the custard over everything.

6   Bake on the center oven rack until the quiche is lightly browned and solid—not soupy—in the center, 45 to 50 minutes; probe it with a paring knife to check. (If you're using the Parmesan cheese, sprinkle it over the top of the quiche about midway through the baking. Expect a nice little bit of extra browning.) Transfer the quiche to a rack and cool for at least 30 minutes before slicing. I prefer waiting an hour; I think it improves the texture.

How to Handle a Leek

Leeks are often grown in sandy soil and present something of a challenge when it comes to cleaning them thoroughly. Start by cutting off and discarding the dark green upper portion of the leek. That section is tough and typically not used except for making stock. Now trim off the little beard at the root end, but don't cut into the leek proper. Next take your chef's knife and cut through the leek lengthwise, leaving the very end—where the beard was—intact. Give the leek a quarter turn and make another lengthwise cut. These cuts will leave you with four equal sections and will expose the inner areas of the leek. Holding the leek under running water, carefully fan out the sections to rinse them thoroughly. Your leeks are now ready to be chopped. For this recipe, and many others, slice them into ⅛- to ¼-inch-wide pieces.

LEEK & BACON QUICHE

This is one of my wife's favorite quiches, and a nice way to showcase leeks, a vastly underused vegetable in the American kitchen. We keep the filling simple and let the mild leek, cheese, and bacon flavors create a pure and delicious harmony. **Makes 8 servings**

1 recipe Go-To Pie Dough (page 22), refrigerated

FILLING

3 tablespoons unsalted butter

3 large leeks (white and pale green parts only), finely chopped (see opposite)

5 or 6 slices bacon

4 large eggs

1 cup half-and-half or light cream

⅓ cup heavy cream

2 teaspoons Dijon mustard

¼ teaspoon dried thyme

2 cups grated fontina cheese

1   If you haven't already, prepare the pastry and refrigerate it for at least 1½ to 2 hours.

2   On a lightly floured sheet of wax paper, roll the dough into a 13- to 13½-inch circle. Invert the pastry over a 9½- to 10-inch tart pan, center it, then peel off the paper. Gently tuck the pastry into the pan without stretching it, and sculpt the edge into an upstanding ridge. Refrigerate the shell for 1 hour, then partially prebake and cool according to the directions on page 18. Preheat the oven to 375°F.

3   Melt the butter in a large skillet over medium heat. Add the leeks and sauté gently, stirring often, until good and soft, 8 or 9 minutes. Cover the pan occasionally, if necessary, to trap the moisture and keep the leeks lubricated. (They scorch easily.) Transfer the leeks to a plate and set aside.

4   Put the skillet back on the heat and add the bacon. Cook until crisp, then transfer the bacon to another plate and set aside.

5   Whisk the eggs in a large bowl until blended. Whisk in the half-and-half, heavy cream, mustard, thyme, ¾ teaspoon salt, and ¼ teaspoon ground black pepper. Set aside.

6   Spread the leeks evenly in the tart shell. Top with 1 cup of the fontina cheese. Slowly pour the custard over everything. Sprinkle on the remaining 1 cup cheese, then crumble the bacon over the top.

7   Bake the quiche on the center oven rack until golden brown and puffy, 35 to 45 minutes. Transfer to a rack and cool for at least 30 minutes before slicing.

Recipe for Success

Fontina cheese has just the perfectly mild and nutty flavor to complement the delicate leeks. However, feel free to use another mild melting cheese if that's what you have on hand.

CARAMELIZED ONION, BACON & SWISS CHEESE PIE

Here's a quiche with layer upon layer of deep, rich flavors: caramelized onions and garlic sautéed in bacon fat; sharp Swiss or Gruyère cheese; and a generous dollop of Dijon mustard, one of the key ingredients in many of my quiche recipes. It's good any time of year, but I tend to think of this as the perfect pie for a chilly winter day. **Makes 8 to 10 servings**

1 recipe Go-To Pie Dough (page 22), refrigerated

FILLING

4 or 5 slices bacon, cut crosswise into ½-inch pieces

6 to 7 cups halved and thinly sliced sweet onions (2 to 3 large)

3 garlic cloves, minced

5 large eggs

1 cup half-and-half

½ cup heavy cream

2 tablespoons all-purpose flour

Scant 1 tablespoon Dijon mustard

1 teaspoon dried thyme

2 to 3 cups grated Swiss or Gruyère cheese

1   If you haven't already, prepare the pastry and refrigerate it for at least 1½ to 2 hours.

2   On a lightly floured sheet of wax paper, roll the dough into a 13- to 13½-inch circle. Invert the pastry over a 9½-inch deep-dish pie pan or a similar-size tart pan, center it, then peel off the paper. Gently tuck the pastry into the pan without stretching it, and sculpt the edge into an upstanding ridge. Refrigerate the shell for 1 hour, then partially prebake and cool according to the directions on page 18. Preheat the oven to 375°F.

3   Heat a large, heavy skillet over medium heat and add the bacon. Fry until crisp. Using a slotted spoon, transfer the bacon to a plate. Leave enough bacon fat in the pan to coat the bottom thickly (see Recipe for Success).

4   Add the onions to the skillet and sauté, partially covered, until they're a rich golden brown, about 20 minutes. Stir in the garlic for the last couple of minutes. Remove from the heat.

5   Whisk the eggs in a large bowl just until frothy. Whisk in the half-and-half, heavy cream, flour, mustard, thyme, ½ teaspoon salt, and ¼ teaspoon ground black pepper.

6   To assemble the pie, spread the sautéed onions evenly in the pie shell. Top with the reserved bacon and about half of the Swiss cheese. Whisk the custard again, then gently ladle it over the filling. Sprinkle the remaining cheese on top.

7   Bake on the center oven rack for 15 minutes. Reduce the temperature to 350°F and continue to bake until the filling is set, about 30 minutes more. If the top hasn't browned to your liking, run the pie briefly under the broiler. Watch it carefully. Transfer the pie to a cooling rack. Serve warm, at room temperature, or cold.

Recipe for Success

If it looks like you have more bacon fat in the pan than you'll need, pour off some into a glass measuring cup and add it back, as the onions sauté, only if needed. It's hard to add too many sliced onions to this pie. It might look like a lot before you cook them, but they'll cook down to a fraction of their size.

It takes a while to get the onions good and golden brown. Don't try to rush it by turning the heat up too high; you'll only scorch them. Take your time.

ALL-IN-ONE BREAKFAST QUICHE

All-in-one because this is everything you want for breakfast—sausage, eggs, and potatoes—all in one crust. Great for anytime you're expecting a crowd for brunch. **Makes 8 servings**

1 recipe Go-To Pie Dough (page 22), refrigerated

FILLING

2 cups diced peeled red-skinned potatoes

8 ounces breakfast sausage links (see Recipe for Success)

2 tablespoons unsalted butter

1 medium onion, chopped

½ green bell pepper, diced

½ teaspoon paprika

4 large eggs

1½ cups light cream or half-and-half

1½ tablespoons all-purpose flour

2 teaspoons Dijon mustard

1 teaspoon crumbled dried sage

1½ cups grated sharp or extra-sharp cheddar cheese

1   If you haven't already, prepare the pastry and refrigerate it for at least 1½ to 2 hours.

2   On a lightly floured sheet of wax paper, roll the dough into a 13- to 13½-inch circle. Invert the pastry over a 9½-inch deep-dish pie pan or a similar-size tart pan, center it, then peel off the paper. Gently tuck the pastry into the pan without stretching it, and sculpt the edge into an upstanding ridge. Refrigerate the shell for 1 hour, then partially prebake and cool according to the directions on page 18. Preheat the oven to 350°F.

3   Put the diced potatoes in a medium saucepan with enough salted water to cover by an inch. Bring to a boil over medium-high heat, then reduce the heat to a low boil and cook the potatoes until just barely tender, 7 to 10 minutes. Drain the potatoes, then spread them on a plate to cool.

4   If you're using fully cooked sausage, cut the links into bite-size chunks. Otherwise, cook the sausage in a large skillet according to the package instructions. Transfer to a plate to cool, then cut into bite-size chunks. Set aside.

5   Melt the butter in the same skillet over medium heat, then stir in the onion and bell pepper. Sauté the vegetables until the onions are translucent, about 10 minutes. Add the paprika and potatoes and cook for 1 minute, stirring often so everything is well coated with the seasoning. Remove from the heat and set aside.

6   Whisk the eggs in a large bowl until blended. Add the cream, flour, mustard, sage, ¾ teaspoon salt, and ground black pepper to taste. Whisk well.

Continued

7   Spread the vegetables evenly in the pie shell. Scatter the sausage chunks here and there, and top all that with 1 cup of the cheese. Whisk the custard again, then pour it slowly into the shell. Top with the remaining ½ cup cheese.

8   Bake the quiche until light brown and puffy on top and set in the middle, 45 to 55 minutes. Transfer to a rack and cool for at least 30 minutes before serving.

Recipe for Success

Regarding your choice of a breakfast sausage, opt for one with a little extra punch of flavor, such as spicy, maple, or sage. It'll give the quiche a more authentic breakfast flavor.

There's a bit of prep involved with this quiche, but plenty of opportunity, also, to do some of it ahead. At the very least, you can make and prebake the shell the day before, cook the potatoes, and chop the vegetables. That will give you a real jump on the dish the next morning.

BROCCOLI, MUSHROOM & HAM QUICHE

Broccoli must have been the default filling when quiche mania first started sweeping the country, because it's still the first quiche many people think of when the subject comes up. One taste, and you'll understand why it caught on: All of the flavors meld perfectly. And with such a hearty blend of veggies and protein, one slice makes a meal. **Makes 8 servings**

1 recipe Go-To Pie Dough (page 22), refrigerated

FILLING

3 tablespoons unsalted butter

1 medium onion, chopped

1 cup sliced white mushroom caps

1 garlic clove, minced

3 to 4 cups small broccoli florets

4 large eggs

¾ cup whole milk

⅔ cup heavy cream

1½ tablespoons all-purpose flour

1 tablespoon Dijon mustard

2 cups grated sharp or extra-sharp cheddar cheese

1 cup diced ham

1   If you haven't already, prepare the pastry and refrigerate it for at least 1½ to 2 hours.

2   On a lightly floured sheet of wax paper, roll the dough into a 13- to 13½-inch circle. Invert the pastry over a 9½-inch deep-dish pie pan or a similar-size tart pan, center it, then peel off the paper. Gently tuck the pastry into the pan without stretching it, and sculpt the edge into an upstanding ridge. Refrigerate the shell for 1 hour, then partially prebake and cool according to the directions on page 18. Preheat the oven to 375°F.

3   Melt the butter in a large skillet over medium heat. Stir in the onion and mushrooms and cook for 10 minutes. Stir in the garlic and broccoli; salt everything lightly. Reduce the heat to low and cook until the broccoli is starting to lose its crunch, 3 to 5 minutes. Remove from the heat.

4   Whisk the eggs in a large bowl just until frothy. Whisk in the milk, cream, flour, mustard, ½ teaspoon salt, and ¼ teaspoon ground black pepper.

5   Spread the contents of the skillet evenly in the pie shell. Cover with 1 cup of the cheese and all of the ham. Briefly whisk the custard again, then slowly pour it over the solids. Cover with the remaining 1 cup cheese. Bake the quiche on the center oven rack for 15 minutes. Reduce the heat to 350°F and continue to bake until the quiche is set, slightly puffy, and golden, 25 to 30 minutes. Cool for at least 30 minutes before slicing and serving.

Recipe for Success

Minus the ham, this becomes a vegetarian quiche extraordinaire. Double the amount of sliced mushrooms if you nix the ham.

SMOKY BACON & CHEDDAR CHEESE QUICHE

Think of this as a renegade version of quiche Lorraine, equally rich and bacon laced, but with a few personal liberties—like smoked paprika and extra-sharp cheddar—that would make a French cook blanch, or perhaps bristle. And yet, it's hard to argue with the great taste. Unlike some of the quiches here, this one has fewer add-ins, so there's more savory custard per forkful. If you can appreciate that, put this one near the top of your quiche bucket list. **Makes 8 servings**

1 recipe Go-To Pie Dough (page 22), refrigerated

FILLING

4 slices bacon

1 medium onion, chopped

1 teaspoon smoked paprika

5 large eggs

¾ cup heavy cream

¾ cup whole milk

½ teaspoon Dijon mustard

1½ cups grated extra-sharp cheddar cheese

1   If you haven't already, prepare the pastry and refrigerate it for at least 1½ to 2 hours.

2   On a lightly floured sheet of wax paper, roll the dough into a 13- to 13½-inch circle. Invert the pastry over a 9½-inch deep-dish pie pan or a similar-size tart pan, center it, then peel off the paper. Gently tuck the pastry into the pan without stretching it, and sculpt the edge into an upstanding ridge. Refrigerate the shell for 1 hour, then partially prebake and cool according to the directions on page 18. Preheat the oven to 375°F.

3   Heat a large skillet over medium heat and add the bacon. Fry until crisp. Transfer the bacon to a plate, leaving about 3 tablespoons of bacon fat in the pan. Stir in the onion and sauté until soft and translucent, 7 to 8 minutes. Stir in the smoked paprika, mixing it well with the onions, then immediately remove the pan from the heat.

4   Whisk the eggs in a large bowl just until frothy. Whisk in the heavy cream, milk, mustard, ½ teaspoon salt, and ground black pepper to taste. Stir in the cheddar cheese, about half at a time. Finally, scrape the onions out of the skillet and stir them into the custard mixture.

5   Slowly pour the custard into the partially prebaked shell. Place on the center oven rack and bake for 20 minutes. Reduce the heat to 350°F and continue to bake until set in the middle, 20 to 25 minutes more. Transfer to a rack and cool for at least 30 minutes before slicing and serving.

Recipe for Success

If you want to spend an enjoyable 30 minutes online, Google Julia Child's 1963 show, *The French Chef*, and find the episode where she makes a quiche Lorraine. I did, in part because I wanted to see how she handled the bacon (which she simmered, to defat before frying) and in part because it's just good old-fashioned cooking entertainment. She describes quiche as if most of her audience wasn't familiar with it, which was indeed the case at that time. And she bakes the quiche in a traditional flan ring. It all looks so quaint: no massive kitchen or $10,000 range like you see with today's TV chefs. It's just a simple home kitchen setup, but one where she taught generations how to prepare wonderful food.

Even though I don't specify it, white cheddar is more or less my default choice for cheddar. Many orange cheddars are, of course, excellent in quality. But I've always had a hard time disassociating the color orange from cheap imitation cheese. I realize that's my problem, not yours, and I should probably just get over it. But I did think it was worth mentioning.

ITALIAN SAUSAGE & SPINACH POLENTA PIE

Over the years, I've developed a number of quiche and dinner pie recipes built on a foundation of polenta, or what's commonly known in this country as cornmeal mush. Blend eggs and seasonings into this base, dress it up with cheese and other interesting add-ins, and you wind up with a quiche whose texture is something like a soft take on firm polenta. It works very nicely in a quiche, particularly one with lots of spinach and hot Italian sausage. The pie is good on its own, but it shines with a little tomato something on the side: chunky tomato sauce, roasted tomatoes (see page 126), or plain sliced tomatoes in season. **Makes 8 servings**

1 recipe Go-To Pie Dough (page 22), refrigerated

FILLING

2 tablespoons olive oil

1 medium onion, halved and thinly sliced

8 ounces hot Italian sausage meat, out of the casing

8 ounces baby spinach

1¾ cups whole milk

⅓ cup fine yellow cornmeal

1 cup grated fontina, sharp cheddar, or other melting cheese

⅓ cup grated Parmesan cheese

3 large eggs, lightly beaten

1   If you haven't already, prepare the pastry and refrigerate it for at least 1½ to 2 hours.

2   On a lightly floured sheet of wax paper, roll the dough into a 13- to 13½-inch circle. Invert the pastry over a 9½-inch deep-dish pie pan or a similar-size tart pan, center it, then peel off the paper. Gently tuck the pastry into the pan without stretching it, and sculpt the edge into an upstanding ridge. Refrigerate the shell for 1 hour, then partially prebake and cool according to the directions on page 18. Preheat the oven to 375°F.

3   Heat the olive oil in a large skillet over medium heat and stir in the onion. Sauté for 3 to 4 minutes, then add the sausage in bite-size chunks. Cook for 5 to 6 minutes longer, then add the spinach; salt lightly. Continue to cook until the sausage is done and the spinach is wilted, 4 to 5 more minutes. Remove from the heat and set aside.

4   Combine the milk and cornmeal in a medium saucepan, preferably nonstick. Gradually bring to a low boil over medium heat, whisking often, and cook until slightly thickened, about 5 minutes. Remove from the heat and scrape into a large mixing bowl. Stir in the cheeses, a handful at a time. Cool for 10 minutes.

5   Add the eggs to the cornmeal mixture; whisk until thoroughly blended. Whisk in ½ teaspoon salt and ground black pepper to taste. Stir in the spinach and sausage mixture.

6   Slowly pour the filling into the partially prebaked shell; smooth with a spoon. Bake on the center oven rack until the top is golden brown and slightly puffed, 40 to 45 minutes. Poke the center with a paring knife; there should be no evidence of uncooked custard when it's done. Transfer to a rack and cool for at least 30 minutes before slicing.

Recipe for Success

If I can find it, I like to use bulk Italian sausage meat. It saves the (admittedly small) step of squeezing the meat out of the casings, but it's a small time saver that I welcome.

Be sure to use a fine-textured yellow cornmeal here, like Quaker brand. It yields a smoother result than coarse ground cornmeal.

Don't let the firm skin that forms on the surface of the pie fool you into thinking it is done. You really have to probe the pie with a paring knife to be sure.

POT PIES

VEGETABLE POT PIE
WITH A PUMPKIN BISCUIT CRUST

One of my first professional cooking jobs was head cook and bottle washer at a group home for kids, where everyone—and every meal—was vegetarian. It was an ongoing challenge finding dishes that pleased all the kids and staff, but whenever I would make versions of this meatless pot pie I knew there would be only compliments. It's that delicious. **Makes 6 servings**

1 recipe Pumpkin-Sage Biscuit Crust (page 36), prepared as instructed in step 1

FILLING

4 tablespoons (½ stick) unsalted butter, plus 2 tablespoons additional melted butter for the biscuits

2 leeks (white and pale green parts only), chopped (see page 130)

2 celery ribs, thinly sliced

1 smallish green or red bell pepper, seeded and chopped

8 ounces white mushroom caps, sliced

1 carrot, peeled and cut into thin rounds

3 cups vegetable broth

2 cups peeled and cubed winter squash

1½ cups frozen green peas (no need to thaw)

1 medium potato, peeled and cut into large dice

1½ tablespoons tomato paste

¾ teaspoon dried thyme

½ teaspoon dried sage

1 bay leaf

¼ cup all-purpose flour

½ cup light cream or half-and-half

½ cup grated Parmesan cheese

1   Prepare the biscuits as instructed, but don't add the liquid to the dry ingredients quite yet. Refrigerate both the dry and liquid ingredients.

2   Melt the 4 tablespoons butter in a large stovetop casserole over medium heat. Stir in the leeks, celery, bell pepper, mushrooms, and carrot. Salt lightly, then cover and cook for 3 to 4 minutes, allowing liquid to build in the pan. Uncover the pan and cook the vegetables, stirring often, until everything is soft and the leeks are starting to turn golden, another 8 minutes or so.

Collect Those Cutters

In a number of recipes in this collection, you're instructed to use a round cutter of a certain size. Do you keep cutters on hand? You should. It's such a basic kitchen tool, and I can't tell you how many times I reach for my cutters in a given week. I use them for biscuits, for tartlets, to make a small hole in the center of a large top crust—the list goes on. I even have specialized cutters for when I want a chicken silhouette to top a chicken pot pie, or a pig when there's sausage in the filling. Still others I use when I want to put an autumn leaf in the center of a fall fruit pie. So collect those cutters. You can pick up a graduated round set for just a few dollars and, if you do much baking at all, you'll eventually use all of them. That's what I call a good investment.

Continued

3   Add the vegetable broth, winter squash, peas, and potato to the casserole. Bring to a simmer, stirring in the tomato paste, thyme, sage, and bay leaf, plus ¼ teaspoon salt—or more if your broth is not salty—and ground black pepper to taste. Reduce the heat, cover, and simmer the mixture gently, stirring occasionally, until the winter squash is very soft and starting to fall apart, anywhere from 10 to 20 minutes. The potatoes should be tender. Preheat the oven to 400°F.

4   Transfer two or three ladles full of broth to a small bowl. Add the flour and whisk until smooth. Stir this thickener back into the pot and continue to simmer, stirring often, for about 5 minutes. Stir in the cream and cook at a very low simmer for 5 minutes more. Remove from the heat. Taste and see if you need more salt and pepper.

5   Transfer the filling to a deepish, medium-size casserole; the filling should not come any closer than 1 inch to the top rim.

6   Finish mixing the biscuits, patting them out so they're slightly more than ½ inch thick. Using a 2- or 2¼-inch round cutter, cut the dough and gently place the rounds, evenly spaced, on top of the filling. Brush the tops with the remaining 2 tablespoons melted butter, then sprinkle the Parmesan cheese over them.

7   Bake on the center oven rack until the biscuits are crusty and golden, about 25 minutes. Transfer to a rack and cool for at least 10 minutes before serving.

Recipe for Success

I often like to break up the preparation when I'm making an ambitious dish; here's how I do it for this one. I prepare the filling the day before and transfer it to the casserole dish I'm going to bake and serve it in. Then I cover it and refrigerate overnight. The next day, I put the cold casserole in a 375°F oven about 30 minutes before I make the biscuits, stirring it once or twice. Once it comes to a bubble, I increase the heat to 400°F, add the biscuits, and finish baking.

OLD BAY SEAFOOD POT PIE

A really good seafood pot pie is one of the most memorable dinner pies you can create. We begin with steamed mussels, in part for the meats but also for the lovely broth. Next we'll simmer shrimp in that broth, thicken the liquid with a buttery roux, and build flavor with aromatic vegetables and Old Bay. Lastly, we'll bulk up the filling with peas and potatoes, add a flaky pastry, and bake to perfection. This is a dish to make when you're not feeling pressed. Take your time, and settle in for a few hours of delightful puttering. **Makes 4 to 6 servings**

1 recipe Go-To Pie Dough (page 22), divided as instructed in step 1 and refrigerated

FILLING

2 pounds mussels, scrubbed and debearded (see below)

½ cup dry white wine

About 2 cups bottled clam juice

8 ounces large shrimp, peeled and deveined

4 tablespoons (½ stick) unsalted butter

1 medium onion, finely chopped

1 celery rib, chopped

8 ounces white mushroom caps, sliced

2 or 3 garlic cloves, minced

⅓ cup all-purpose flour

2¼ teaspoons Old Bay Seasoning

⅓ cup half-and-half

1 cup peeled and finely diced red-skinned potato

1 cup frozen green peas (no need to thaw)

¼ to ½ cup canned or fresh diced tomatoes

1 egg beaten with 1 tablespoon milk

1   Prepare the dough as instructed, dividing it into four to six equal pieces, depending on the size of the individual pot pie dishes you'll be using (they should each have a capacity of 1 to 1¼ cups). The pastry will be used for the top crust—there is no bottom crust—so unless your dishes are more than, say, 5 inches wide, you can probably get six out of a single batch of dough. Wrap each piece of dough in plastic wrap and refrigerate for at least 1½ hours. While the dough chills, butter your pot pie dishes and set them aside.

2   Put the mussels in a large pot and add the wine. Cover and bring to a boil over medium-high heat, then steam the mussels for 5 to 7 minutes. Using a slotted spoon, transfer the mussels to a large bowl and set aside to cool, reserving their cooking broth. Discard any that haven't opened.

Mussels Know-How

Whenever possible, I like to prepare mussels the same day I buy them, because freshness is everything when it comes to seafood. To ready mussels for cooking, first scrub them under running water with a firm brush to remove loose grit. If any of the mussels are partially open, tap with a finger: They should close up. If not, discard, along with any others with damaged or partially missing shells. Use scissors to cut off any hairy little beards that are attached. After they've steamed, discard any mussels that haven't opened.

Continued

3   Line a colander with cheesecloth and place it inside another bowl. Pour the mussel broth through it to strain out any particles, then pour the strained liquid into a 2-cup measuring cup. Set aside. When the mussels are cool enough to handle, pick the meats from the shells (discard the shells) and set aside.

4   Rinse the original pot and put it back on the stove. Add enough clam juice to the mussel broth to make 2 cups. Pour these 2 cups into the pot, then add another ½ cup clam juice. Bring to a simmer over medium heat and add the shrimp. Cover and poach just until the shrimp are opaque and cooked through, 2 to 3 minutes. Pour the broth and shrimp into a bowl and set aside. Put the pot back on the stove over medium heat.

5   Melt the butter in the pot, then stir in the onion, celery, and mushrooms. Cook the vegetables until the onions are translucent, 5 to 6 minutes, then stir in the garlic, flour, and Old Bay. Cook, stirring, for 1 minute, then add the shrimp and broth. Cook for several minutes, stirring, until the sauce thickens. Add the half-and-half and simmer gently for a minute or two. Remove from the heat. Preheat the oven to 375°F.

6   Put the potatoes and peas in a small saucepan. Add enough lightly salted water to barely cover. Bring to a boil over medium-high heat, then reduce the heat and cook at a low boil until the potatoes are just tender, 7 or 8 minutes. Drain.

7   Taste the creamy fish sauce; add salt and pepper to taste. Add the mussels, potatoes, peas, and tomatoes. Divide the filling evenly among the buttered dishes.

8   Working with one piece of dough at a time (and leaving the others in the refrigerator), roll the pastry so it is slightly larger than the diameter of the dish. Place the pastry over the filling, tucking it down between the filling and dish. (You can also roll the pastry even a little bigger, and drape it over the sides of the dish.) Poke a steam vent in the top with a paring knife. Repeat for the other pot pies.

9   Place the dishes on a large baking sheet. Lightly brush the pastry with the egg wash. Bake the pies on the center oven rack until the filling is bubbly and the tops are golden brown, about 40 minutes. Transfer the dishes to a rack and cool for at least 10 minutes before serving.

Recipe for Success

The filling can be made earlier in the day and divided up, then refrigerated, and the pastry can be made a day or two ahead. However, the pot pies should be assembled and baked the same day.

If you prefer clams over mussels, those will work fine in this recipe, too.

SHRIMP POT PIE

These pot pies are rich and creamy, with little to distract from their right-off-the-trawler taste of fresh shrimp. The portions may be small, but the flavor payoff is huge—the perfect dish to celebrate a seaside getaway, even if it's just the one in your dreams. **Makes 4 to 6 servings**

1 recipe Go-To Pie Dough (page 22), divided as instructed in step 1 and refrigerated

FILLING

3 tablespoons unsalted butter

8 ounces large shrimp, peeled and deveined

1 leek (white and pale green parts only), finely chopped (see page 130), or 1 small onion, finely chopped

3 garlic cloves

1 celery rib, finely chopped

1 medium carrot, peeled and finely diced

8 ounces thinly sliced white mushroom caps

1 tablespoon all-purpose flour

½ teaspoon smoked paprika

1½ cups half-and-half

½ cup heavy cream

¼ teaspoon dried thyme

1 egg yolk beaten with 1 tablespoon milk

1   Prepare the dough as instructed, dividing it into four to six equal pieces, depending on the size of the individual pot pie dishes you'll be using (they should each have a capacity of 1 to 1¼ cups). The pastry will be used for the top crust—there is no bottom crust—so unless your dishes are more than, say, 5 inches wide, you can probably get six out of a single batch of dough. Wrap each piece of dough in plastic wrap and refrigerate for at least 1½ hours. While the dough chills, butter your pot pie dishes and set them aside.

2   Melt the butter in a large stovetop casserole over medium heat. Add the shrimp and cook for 1 minute on each side. Transfer the shrimp to a plate to cool—they won't be fully cooked yet. When cool, cut each shrimp into two or three bite-size pieces.

3   Add the leek, garlic, celery, carrot, and mushrooms to the pan. Salt and pepper lightly. Cover the pan and sweat the vegetables for about 5 minutes, stirring occasionally. Stir in the flour and smoked paprika. Cook for 1 minute, stirring, then add the half-and-half. Bring to a gentle simmer and, as the filling starts to thicken, stir in the heavy cream, thyme, ¼ teaspoon salt, and the shrimp. Simmer gently for several more minutes, then taste again and add more salt and pepper as needed. Remove the pan from the heat, divide the filling evenly among the buttered pans, and cool (see Recipe for Success).

4 When you're ready to bake the pies, preheat the oven to 375°F. Put a large baking sheet on the center oven rack to preheat along with the oven.

5 Working with one piece of dough at a time (and leaving the others in the refrigerator), roll it out about 1 inch larger than the diameter of your pie dish. Drape the dough over the filling and pan, letting it hang down the sides. Using a paring knife, make a small steam vent in the pastry. Repeat for the rest of the pies. Lightly brush the pastry with the egg wash.

6 Place the pies on the baking sheet in the oven and bake until the top crust is golden brown, about 35 minutes. Don't overbake; you don't want all the flavorful sauce to dry up. Transfer the pies to a cooling rack and cool for about 10 minutes before serving.

Recipe for Success

This is another one of those cases where I like to get the filling as cool as I can before baking. If the filling is still hot or even warm when these begin to bake, it will bubble and boil and lose much of its sauciness before the pastry is fully baked. The best tactic is this: After the filling comes off the heat, immediately ladle it into your individual pie pans. Cool to lukewarm, then put them in the fridge for about an hour (or more; this is a great do-ahead step if you want to do most of the work in advance). Finally, roll the pastry, drape it over the top, and bake.

TUNA BAKE POT PIE

Part pot pie, part classic tuna-noodle casserole, this hearty cold weather dish satisfies to the core. We use whole wheat elbow noodles to give this a wholesome profile, but only about a third as many as you'd use in a casserole, in order to keep the filling good and saucy. For the veggies I usually reach for a bag of frozen peas, or peas and carrots if I have them on hand. Serve with something lean and green, like a salad or thinly sliced cucumbers dressed with vinaigrette. **Makes 4 to 6 servings**

1 recipe Cornmeal Pie Dough (page 28) or Go-To Pie Dough (page 22), divided as instructed in step 1 and refrigerated

FILLING

1 cup whole wheat elbow noodles

1¼ cups frozen peas or mixed peas and carrots (no need to thaw)

3 tablespoons unsalted butter

½ large onion, finely chopped

2½ tablespoons all-purpose flour

1 teaspoon Old Bay Seasoning or other seafood seasoning

2⅔ cups whole milk

4 ounces cream cheese, cut into tablespoon-size pieces

1 teaspoon Dijon mustard

1 (5-ounce) can oil-packed tuna, undrained, flaked

1½ cups grated extra-sharp cheddar cheese

1   Prepare the dough as instructed, dividing it into four to six equal pieces, depending on the size of the individual pot pie dishes you'll be using (they should each have a capacity of 1 to 1¼ cups). The pastry will be used for the top crust—there is no bottom crust—so unless your dishes are more than, say, 5 inches wide, you can probably get six out of a single batch of dough. Wrap each piece of dough in plastic wrap and refrigerate for at least 1½ hours. While the dough chills, butter your pot pie dishes and set them aside.

2   Bring a large saucepan of salted water to a boil over high heat. Stir in the noodles and cook for only about half the time recommended on the package. Add the frozen peas, return to a boil, and continue to cook until the noodles are just about fully tender. Drain, then transfer the noodles and vegetables to a large bowl.

3   Melt the butter in a large skillet over medium heat. Add the onion and sauté for about 7 minutes. Stir in the flour and Old Bay and cook, stirring, for 1 minute. Stir in the milk, about 1 cup at a time, waiting until the mixture thickens before adding the next portion. Add the cream cheese, mustard, and ½ teaspoon salt and whisk gently until smooth and creamy. Remove from the heat.

4   Add the tuna and cheddar cheese to the noodles and vegetables. Add the sauce and mix well; it will be on the soupy side. Taste and add salt or pepper as necessary. Divide the filling among the buttered dishes (see Recipe for Success). Let cool for about 15 minutes while you preheat the oven to 375°F.

5   Working with one piece of dough at a time (and leaving the others in the refrigerator), roll the pastry a little larger than the diameter of the pie dish. Drape the pastry over the filling and the sides of the dish. Poke the center of the pastry with a paring knife to make a steam vent. Repeat for the other pot pies. If you have a large enough baking sheet, line it with parchment paper or foil and bake them on the sheet. Or bake them directly on the center oven rack. Either way, they'll be done in about 35 minutes, when the filling is good and bubbly and the pastry is golden. Cool on a rack for at least 10 minutes before serving.

Recipe for Success

When dividing the filling, make sure you have a fairly equal proportion of sauce to solids in each pie dish. You don't want a bunch of sauce in one and mainly noodles and veggies in another.

The tuna flavor is pretty subtle with just one can. Add a second can if you want to enhance the tuna taste.

CURRIED CHICKEN POT PIE

This is my favorite chicken pot pie recipe. The flavor and texture are perfect, and everyone who tries this asks how I make it. Now you know. **Makes 4 to 6 servings**

1 recipe Go-To Pie Dough (page 22), divided as instructed in step 1 and refrigerated

FILLING

4 tablespoons (½ stick) unsalted butter

½ large onion, chopped

1 large carrot, peeled and finely diced

1 medium red bell pepper, seeded and finely diced

¼ cup all-purpose flour

2 tablespoons curry powder

1¾ cups chicken broth

1¼ cups half-and-half or whole milk

3 cups chopped cooked chicken

1 cup rinsed and drained canned chickpeas

1 cup frozen green peas (no need to thaw)

⅓ cup canned pumpkin puree (not pumpkin pie filling)

1 egg beaten with 1 tablespoon milk

1   Prepare the dough as instructed, dividing it into four to six equal pieces, depending on the size of the individual pot pie dishes you'll be using (they should each have a capacity of 1 to 1¼ cups). The pastry will be used for the top crust—there is no bottom crust—so unless your dishes are more than, say, 5 inches wide, you can probably get six out of a single batch of dough. Wrap each piece of dough in plastic wrap and refrigerate for at least 1½ hours. While the dough chills, butter your pot pie dishes and set them aside.

2   Melt the butter in a large, heavy stockpot over medium heat. Add the onion, carrot, and bell pepper. Cook until soft, 6 to 7 minutes, then add the flour and curry powder. Stir and cook for another minute, then add the chicken broth and continue to stir until the mixture thickens. Add the half-and-half, return to a simmer, and cook gently for several minutes, allowing the liquid to thicken a bit. Stir in the chicken, chickpeas, peas, and pumpkin and return to a simmer. Simmer the curry for about 5 more minutes.

3   Taste the curry for seasoning. Depending on the saltiness of your broth, you'll probably need to add at least ¼ teaspoon salt—and perhaps twice that. As for the pepper, that will depend on how hot your curry powder is. This is the time to correct your seasoning. Your curry should be well seasoned and saucy, with a good bit of body. Divide the curry evenly among the buttered pie pans. Cool for 20 to 30 minutes while you preheat the oven to 375°F.

4 When you're ready to bake, put a large baking sheet on the center oven rack and let it heat for a few minutes before you put the pot pies in. Working with one piece of dough at a time (and leaving the others in the refrigerator), roll it just slightly larger than the diameter of the pie dish. Prick the center with a fork, then drape the pastry over one of the pans, tucking it down next to the filling around the edge. Repeat for the other pot pies. Lightly brush the top of each one with a little of the egg wash.

5 Place the pot pies on the baking sheet in the oven and bake until they're a rich golden brown and the filling is bubbling hot, 35 to 40 minutes. Transfer to a rack and cool for at least 15 minutes before serving.

Recipe for Success

One of the tricks here is knowing your curry powder or, more to the point, how hot it is. I used a pretty good but still standard-issue curry powder from the spice rack of the supermarket, and 2 tablespoons was perfect. If you use a custom blend from another source, 2 tablespoons might be too much (that is, too hot). If in doubt, err on the side of caution and start with a little less.

The secret ingredient here that gives the curry such a nice, saucy-thick texture is the canned pumpkin. There's just enough of it to add body and leave a faint but pleasant pumpkin flavor, but not enough to obscure the more subtle flavors. You need only ⅓ cup from the can, so plan on making pumpkin bread or muffins, too.

CHICKEN POT PIE
WITH WINTER VEGETABLES

Brussels sprouts may be the most underrated vegetable going, and if you agree then you're probably going to love this version of chicken pot pie. Another twist: Instead of the usual carrots, I use chunks of winter squash. The squash cooks up softer than carrots do, but I think it has all the sweetness and at least as much flavor, so it's a good trade. Mashing the potato and adding it back to the filling makes for a nice thick sauce, delicately flavored with a touch of mustard and thyme. A perfect dinner pie for those coldest of winter days. **Makes 6 servings**

1 recipe Go-To Pie Dough (page 22), refrigerated

FILLING

4 cups chicken broth

1½ cups peeled and diced baking potato

1½ cups quartered Brussels sprouts

1 cup peeled and diced winter squash

3 tablespoons unsalted butter

1 large onion, chopped

3 tablespoons all-purpose flour

3 cups chopped cooked chicken

2 teaspoons Dijon mustard

1 teaspoon dried thyme

1 egg beaten with 1 tablespoon milk

1   If you haven't already, prepare the pastry and refrigerate for at least 1½ hours.

2   Bring the chicken broth to a simmer in a large saucepan over medium-high heat. Add the potato and bring to a low boil. Reduce the heat and simmer, partially covered, until the potato is tender, about 10 minutes. Using a slotted spoon, transfer the potato to a mixing bowl. Add a few tablespoons of the broth and mash with a large fork or masher. Set aside.

3   Bring the liquid back to a very low boil and add the Brussels sprouts. Simmer for 1½ minutes. Add the squash and cook for 2 minutes more. Using a slotted spoon, transfer the vegetables to the bowl with the mashed potatoes. (NOTE: The vegetables won't be tender, just par-cooked.) Reserve the broth.

White Meat or Dark?

Every ad I see for chicken pot pie makes a big deal of the fact that their pie uses only white meat chicken. What's up with that? White meat—breast meat—chicken is great and all, but personally I think the dark meat is more tender and has a better chicken flavor. So I use both in my pot pies. Yes, it's true that dark meat has more fat and calories than white, but the difference is negligible and certainly not enough to worry about unless you're eating legs, wings, and thighs by the bucketful.

Continued

4   Melt the butter in a large, heavy stovetop casserole over medium heat. Add the onion and sauté until soft and translucent, about 8 minutes. Add the flour and cook, stirring, for 1 minute. Stir in 2½ cups of the reserved broth, about half at a time, adding the second portion once the first one thickens up. Stir in the chicken, mustard, thyme, ½ teaspoon salt, and ground black pepper to taste. Stir in all of the reserved vegetables.

5   Simmer the filling for several minutes, adding more broth, if desired, to make the vegetables as saucy as you like. (The sauce shouldn't be too thick because the starch in the potato will continue to thicken it as the pie bakes.) Taste and correct the seasoning. Transfer the filling to an oiled medium-large baking dish. Ideally, the filling should be about 1 inch from the top rim of the casserole. Set aside to cool for 30 minutes while you preheat the oven to 375°F.

6   On a floured work surface, roll the dough out so it is the same shape as your casserole, but just a tad larger. Drape the pastry over the filling, tucking it down between the filling and the dish. Using a paring knife, poke two or three steam vents in the pastry. Lightly brush the pastry with the egg wash. Bake on the center oven rack until the filling is bubbly and the pastry is golden brown, 35 to 40 minutes. Transfer to a rack and cool for at least 15 minutes before serving.

Recipe for Success

One of the tricks to a well-baked pot pie is choosing a casserole that accommodates the filling without being over- or underfilled. If there's too little filling for the pan, the pastry will sit too low and not brown up nicely. If it sits too high in the pan, you run the risk of the filling bubbling over. The best solution is to have a variety of sizes at your disposal. Don't be surprised if—after you've added the filling to the casserole—you decide you actually need a larger (or smaller) one. Happens to me all the time.

THANKSGIVING LEFTOVERS SHEPHERD'S PIE

I love to turn Thanksgiving leftovers into shepherd's pie, partly because it's so easy with all those ingredients just sitting there in the fridge, and partly because it tastes so darn good. It's so easy, in fact, that you scarcely need a recipe, and thus the somewhat free-form feel to this recipe. In a nutshell, we're just chopping up leftover turkey, moistening it with gravy, adding some veggies, spreading it in a pastry shell (you don't even need to prebake it), and slathering mashed potatoes on top. Bake, and that's it. Since your leftovers will stay fresh through the weekend, you can make this on Saturday or even Sunday for a special finale meal for the holiday. **Makes 8 servings**

1 recipe Go-To Pie Dough (page 22), refrigerated

FILLING

3½ to 4 cups chopped cooked turkey

½ cup gravy, warmed

1 to 1½ cups cooked corn, peas, green beans, green bean casserole (see Recipe for Success), or chopped Brussels sprouts, slightly warmed

3½ cups mashed potatoes

Chopped fresh flat-leaf parsley, dried sage, rosemary, and/or thyme (optional)

1 tablespoon cold unsalted butter

Paprika, for dusting the top

1   If you haven't already, prepare the pastry and refrigerate it for at least 1½ hours.

2   On a lightly floured sheet of wax paper, roll the dough into a circle 13 to 13½ inches in diameter. Invert the pastry over a 9½-inch deep-dish pie pan, center it, then peel off the paper. Gently tuck the pastry into the pan without stretching it, and sculpt the edge into an upstanding ridge. Refrigerate the shell for at least 1 hour. Preheat the oven to 375°F.

Recipe for Success

Yes, I'll even use leftover green bean casserole—the classic one with the cream of mushroom soup—in the filling, too. If it's very saucy, I might use a little less gravy in the filling. And I don't mind cutting up the green beans just a little, so they're not out of scale with the rest of the filling ingredients. Oh, the lengths I'll go to for a well-made dinner pie.

Here's a really neat idea if you're feeling adventurous: Crumble a little leftover stuffing into the filling. (Stuffing is my favorite part of the feast.) You don't want to overdo it, but if you cut back a little on the turkey—by no more than a cup—and add that much stuffing instead, it makes for a beautiful pie. Just be sure to break up the stuffing so it gets evenly distributed.

Continued

3   Combine the turkey and gravy in a large mixing bowl. Mix in your choice of leftover vegetables, then add salt and pepper to taste. Stir in ½ cup of the mashed potatoes. Taste. If the filling needs a little flavor boost, add a few big pinches of some of the traditional holiday herbs—parsley, sage, rosemary, and/or thyme. Spread the filling in the refrigerated shell.

4   Warm the remaining 3 cups mashed potatoes just a bit—the microwave is the easiest way—then stir briskly to smooth them out. If they've become quite firm overnight, stir in a few tablespoons hot milk or broth. Smooth evenly over the filling. Dot the potatoes with bits of the butter, then sprinkle a little paprika on top.

5   Bake on the center oven rack until the edge of the pastry is golden brown and the top is well crusted over, about 50 minutes. Transfer to a rack and cool for 20 to 30 minutes before slicing and serving.

TURKEY CRUMB POT PIE

Here's another really good post-Thanksgiving turkey pot pie, but this one has an unusual topping: crumbs made from packaged stuffing mix, and those crispy onions we all love on our green bean casserole. For the veggies, use most anything you have left in the fridge; in a pinch, even thawed frozen vegetables are fine. We make up the sauce as we go, but I'll often enrich the filling with ¼ cup or so of leftover gravy, stirring it in just before the filling comes off the heat. The gravy makes the mixture saucier, but that's seldom a bad thing when you're talking about pot pies. **Makes 4 servings**

1 recipe Go-To Pie Dough (page 22), divided as instructed in step 1 and refrigerated

FILLING

3 tablespoons unsalted butter

½ large onion, finely chopped

1 celery rib or 1 cup sliced white mushroom caps

2½ tablespoons all-purpose flour

2¼ cups chicken broth

¼ cup heavy cream

2½ cups chopped cooked turkey

2 cups cooked vegetables (such as corn, peas, carrots, broccoli, and/or Brussels sprouts), preferably in combination (see Recipe for Success)

½ teaspoon dried sage

½ teaspoon dried thyme

TOPPING

1 cup packaged stuffing mix

1 cup crispy French fried onions

3 tablespoons unsalted butter, melted

1   Prepare the dough as directed, but divide it into four equal balls. Flatten each ball into a ½-inch-thick disk. Wrap the disks individually in plastic wrap and refrigerate for at least 1½ hours. While the dough chills, get out four individual pot pie dishes, each with a capacity of 1 to 1¼ cups, and set them aside.

2   Melt the butter in a large stovetop casserole over medium heat. Add the onion and celery and sauté for 8 minutes. Add the flour and cook, stirring, for another minute. Whisk in the chicken broth. Bring to a simmer, allowing the liquid to thicken a bit, then stir in the cream, turkey, vegetables, sage, thyme, ¼ teaspoon salt, and ground black pepper to taste. Return to a simmer and simmer gently for about 5 minutes. Remove from the heat. Taste, adding more salt as needed. Set aside to cool thoroughly.

3   Working with one piece of dough at a time (and leaving the others in the refrigerator), roll it into a circle about 8 inches in diameter and line one of the pot pie dishes with it. Pinch the edge into an upstanding ridge and flute, if desired. Refrigerate for 30 minutes. Repeat for the rest of the dough. Preheat the oven to 375°F while the shells are chilling.

4   Divide the filling evenly among the pot pie shells. Make sure there's about ½ inch of room between the filling and the top edge of the pastry. Bake on the center oven rack for 30 minutes. (If you have a large enough baking sheet, line the sheet with parchment paper or foil and bake the pies on it, in case of spillovers.)

Continued

5   While the pot pies bake, make the topping. Put the stuffing mix and onions in the bowl of a food processor. Pulse the machine repeatedly, until the mixture is well chopped but still somewhat coarse. Transfer the crumbs to a mixing bowl and add the melted butter. Mix well, and set aside.

6   After the pies have baked for 30 minutes, slide out the oven rack and carefully divide the crumb topping among the pies. Using a fork, spread it around and then press it down gently. Slide the rack back in and continue to bake until the topping browns and the filling is bubbly, 10 to 15 minutes more. Transfer to a rack and cool for 15 to 20 minutes before serving.

Recipe for Success

Another veggie that's good in here is leftover mashed sweet potatoes, but add only a few tablespoons or it will thicken the filling too much. If that happens, or if you simply want to use more of them to stretch the filling, you'll need to thin the filling with a little extra broth.

TACO POT PIE

This is one of my favorite Super Bowl dishes, but I never rule it out on any game day, whether we're tailgating or just sitting in front of the big screen. What we have here is a crunchy cornmeal crust filled with a quick-to-prepare spicy chili and covered with a cheesy ranch blend that turns golden brown and tops off the package beautifully. I love baking these pies in 5-inch-diameter aluminum foil pans. Maybe it's a guy thing, but the disposable pans really jive with the casual nature of this pie. **Makes 4 main-dish or 8 appetizer servings**

1 recipe Cornmeal Pie Dough (page 28), divided as instructed in step 1 and refrigerated

FILLING

2 tablespoons vegetable oil

1 medium onion, finely chopped

1 medium green bell pepper, seeded and finely chopped

1 pound ground beef

8 ounces ground pork

2 garlic cloves, minced

2 tablespoons all-purpose flour

2 teaspoons chili powder

2 teaspoons ground cumin

1 teaspoon smoked paprika

½ teaspoon ground coriander

1¼ cups favorite salsa

1 tablespoon packed brown sugar

1 cup rinsed and drained canned pinto beans

TOPPING

4 ounces cream cheese, at room temperature

½ cup favorite ranch dressing

¼ to ⅓ cup whole milk

1 cup grated extra-sharp cheddar cheese

1   Prepare the cornmeal pastry as instructed, dividing it into four equal balls. Flatten each ball into a ½-inch-thick disk, then wrap the disks individually and refrigerate for 1 to 1½ hours. While the dough chills, get out four individual pie pans, each with a capacity of 1 to 1¼ cups, and set them aside. (This is for main-dish servings; to make appetizer servings, see Recipe for Success.)

2   Working with one piece of dough at a time (and leaving the others in the refrigerator), roll the dough into a 7½- to 8-inch circle on a sheet of lightly floured wax paper. The exact size will depend on your pie pans. Transfer the dough to the pan and press it in gently, taking care not to tear the dough. Roll and pinch the overhang of the dough into an upstanding ridge. Flute or crimp as desired. Refrigerate. Repeat for the other pans, refrigerating those as well.

3   To make the filling, heat the oil in a large skillet over medium heat. Add the onion and bell pepper and sauté for 5 minutes. Add the beef and pork and brown thoroughly, breaking up the meat with a wooden spoon. Remove the pan from the heat, tilt it, and spoon off and discard all but about 3 tablespoons of the fat.

4   Add the garlic, flour, and spices to the meat. Put the skillet back on the heat and cook, stirring, for 1 minute. Stir in the salsa, brown sugar, pinto beans, and a scant ½ teaspoon salt, along with 1 cup water. Bring the mixture to a gentle simmer and cook, partially covered, for about 10 minutes, stirring often. Remove the lid and continue to simmer gently for several minutes more. The mixture should be good and saucy. Remove from the heat, transfer to a bowl, and cool to room temperature. Cover and refrigerate if you're not using it within 30 minutes.

5 When you're ready to bake, adjust your oven rack so it is one position above the bottom shelf. Place a heavy-duty baking sheet on the rack. Preheat the oven to 350°F.

6 While the oven heats up, make the topping. Using an electric mixer, blend the cream cheese in a mixing bowl until smooth. Blend in the ranch dressing. Blend in ¼ cup of the milk; the mixture should have a consistency like thick heavy cream. Use more milk, if needed. Stir in the cheddar cheese by hand. Set aside.

7 Divide the cooled filling among your pie pans, leaving about ½ inch of space between the top of the filling and the top of your pie shell. Smooth with a spoon. Divide the ranch topping among the pies, spreading it evenly over the filling.

8 Place the pot pies on the baking sheet in the oven. Bake for 25 minutes, then carefully move the oven rack and baking sheet to the center of the oven and continue to bake until the topping and the exposed crust are nicely browned, 10 to 15 minutes more. Transfer to a rack and cool for at least 20 minutes before serving.

Recipe for Success

To make appetizer-size pies, you're going to press the dough into muffin cups instead of rolling it. (Pressing is easier when you're using smaller cups.) Divide the dough into eight pieces and place each piece in a buttered standard-size muffin pan cup. Press the dough evenly into the bottom and up the sides of the cup, shaping the dough so it comes ⅛ to ¼ inch above the top of the pan. When they're all pressed in, refrigerate the pan while you make the filling. Proceed as usual, dividing the filling and topping evenly among the shells. These appetizer pies will take about the same amount of time to bake as the larger pies, perhaps a few minutes less. Cool on a rack for about 20 minutes before trying to remove them.

If you do bake these pies in muffin cups, you might want to line your cups with ½-inch-wide strips of wax paper. Make the strips long enough to come about an inch above the pan on each side. You'll be able to lift on these tabs later to loosen and remove the little pies.

SAUSAGE & GUINNESS POT PIE

I love the deep, rich flavor of this saucy pie. It's the sort of hearty dish you'd expect to find in a good Irish pub, accompanied by slabs of grainy bread, a glass of stout, and a round of cheer. Unlike a lot of pot pies with a cast of thousands, this one is all about the sausage and carrots, but if you can't resist, then go ahead and add some peas. **Makes 4 to 6 servings**

1 recipe Go-To Pie Dough (page 22), divided as instructed in step 1 and refrigerated

FILLING

2 tablespoons olive oil or vegetable oil

5 bratwursts (about 1¼ pounds total)

1 large onion, halved and thinly sliced

3 large carrots, peeled and sliced into ¼-inch-thick rounds

4 garlic cloves, minced

3 tablespoons all-purpose flour

1½ cups beef broth

1 cup Guinness or other stout

2 tablespoons Heinz chili sauce

1½ tablespoons tomato paste

1½ tablespoons light brown sugar

1½ teaspoons Worcestershire sauce

1½ cups grated extra-sharp cheddar cheese

1   Prepare the dough as instructed, dividing it into four to six pieces, depending on the size of the individual pot pie dishes you'll be using (they should each have a capacity of 1 to 1¼ cups). The pastry will be used for the top crust—there is no bottom crust—so unless your dishes are more than, say, 5 inches wide, you can probably get six out of a single batch of dough. Wrap each piece of dough in plastic wrap and refrigerate for at least 1½ hours. While the dough chills, butter your pot pie dishes and set them aside.

2   Heat the oil in a large stovetop casserole over medium-high heat. Prick each of the sausages several times with a fork, then add to the pot. Brown for 5 minutes, turning once or twice. Transfer the brats to a plate and set them aside.

3   Add the onion and carrots to the pan. Cook, stirring often, for 4 to 5 minutes. Stir in the garlic and flour. Cook and stir for another 30 seconds, then stir in the beef broth and stout. Bring to a simmer and, as the liquid starts to thicken, stir in the chili sauce, tomato paste, and brown sugar. Slice the brats thickly and add them to the pot. Simmer gently for 10 minutes, then stir in the Worcestershire sauce. Remove from the heat and stir in the cheese. Add salt and pepper to taste. It will likely need at least ¼ teaspoon salt and perhaps even ½ teaspoon or more, depending on the saltiness of your beef broth.

4   Divide the filling evenly among the buttered dishes. Cool for 15 minutes while you preheat the oven to 375°F.

5   Working with one piece of dough at a time (and leaving the others in the refrigerator), roll the pastry a little larger than the diameter of the pie dish. Drape the pastry over the filling and the sides of the dish. Poke the center of the pastry with a paring knife to make a steam vent. Repeat for the other pot pies. If you have a large enough baking sheet, line it with parchment paper or foil and bake them on the sheet. Or bake them directly on the center oven rack. Either way, they'll be done in about 35 minutes, when the filling is good and bubbly and the pastry is golden. Transfer the dishes to a rack and cool for 10 to 15 minutes before serving.

Recipe for Success

Stout alone, without a few choice ingredients to temper the bitterness, is a bit much for my taste. The tomato paste, chili sauce, and brown sugar go a long way in toning down that bitter edge, and the cheddar really mellows out the filling. If you want a more robust, stout-y flavor, you can add less of these ingredients to start, and increase them to your liking.

CLASSIC BEEF POT PIE

Say "beef pot pie" and most folks will imagine something like this: a saucy, aromatic, slow-simmered mélange of beef chunks, carrots, potatoes, and other veggies, delicately seasoned with herbs. And that pretty much says it all. About the only way you can improve on this one is to prepare the filling the day ahead and refrigerate it overnight; stew-like dishes always benefit from this overnight mingling of flavors. **Makes 4 to 6 servings**

1 recipe Go-To Pie Dough (page 22), divided as instructed in step 1 and refrigerated

FILLING

1¼ pounds stew beef, cut into bite-size pieces

½ cup all-purpose flour

4 tablespoons vegetable oil

1 large onion, chopped

2 celery ribs, chopped

2 cups sliced white mushroom caps

2 garlic cloves, minced

3 cups beef broth

½ cup dry red wine

1 bay leaf

1 large baking potato, peeled and cut into ½-inch dice

2 carrots, peeled and diced

1½ cups frozen green peas (no need to thaw)

3 tablespoons tomato paste

1½ tablespoons Worcestershire sauce

1½ tablespoons light brown sugar

1½ teaspoons dried thyme

1 teaspoon dried oregano

¼ cup all-purpose flour

1 egg beaten with 1 tablespoon milk

1   Prepare the dough as instructed, dividing it into four to six equal pieces, depending on the size of the individual pot pie dishes you'll be using (they should each have a capacity of 1 to 1¼ cups). The pastry will be used for the top crust—there is no bottom crust—so unless your dishes are more than, say, 5 inches wide, you can probably get six out of a single batch of dough. Wrap each piece of dough in plastic wrap and refrigerate for at least 1½ hours. While the dough chills, butter your pot pie dishes and set them aside.

2   Combine the beef and flour in a paper bag and shake well. Set aside. Heat 2 tablespoons of the oil in a large, heavy stockpot over medium heat. Shake the excess flour from the meat, then add half of the beef to the hot pan. Let it sit for at least a minute, then stir the meat and continue to brown for another couple of minutes. Transfer the meat to a bowl.

3   Add the remaining 2 tablespoons oil to the pan and add the rest of the meat. Brown as above, then add the onion, celery, mushrooms, and garlic to the pan. Cook for a couple of minutes, stirring often, then return the first batch of meat to the pan. Add the beef broth, wine, bay leaf, and ½ teaspoon salt. Bring to a simmer, then add the potato, carrots, peas, tomato paste, Worcestershire sauce, brown sugar, thyme, and oregano, along with ground black pepper to taste.

4   Bring the mixture back to a simmer, stirring often. Cover and simmer the mixture very gently (don't boil) for about 30 minutes, stirring occasionally, until the potatoes are barely tender. Toward the end of the cooking, taste the broth several times to see if you need more salt or other seasoning.

5   Put the flour in a small mixing bowl and ladle 2 good scoops of the broth into the bowl. Whisk well to smooth it out, then add this thickener back to the pot. Simmer the mixture until the filling has a thickish, saucy consistency, about 5 minutes. Remove from the heat.

6   Spoon the filling into the buttered pie pans and smooth the tops, then set aside to cool for 20 to 30 minutes. Preheat the oven to 375°F.

7   When you're ready to bake, put a large baking sheet on the center oven rack and let it heat for a few minutes before you put the pot pies in. Working with one piece of dough at a time (and leaving the others in the refrigerator), roll it just slightly larger than the diameter of a pie pan. Prick the center with a fork, then drape the pastry over one of the pans, tucking it down next to the filling around the edge. Repeat for the other pot pies. Lightly brush the top of each one with a little of the egg wash.

8   Place the pot pies on the baking sheet in the oven and bake until they're a rich golden brown and the filling is bubbling hot, 35 to 40 minutes. Transfer to a rack and cool for at least 15 minutes before serving.

Recipe for Success

On occasion, I make these up as double crusted pot pies. Here's how to do it: First, make up a double crust batch of the Go-To Pie Dough (page 22). Divide it in half, making one half a little larger than the other, then divide both halves into five equal portions each. Shape the dough portions into disks, then wrap and refrigerate—but be sure to keep them separate in the fridge because the disks from the larger portion of dough will be used for the shells and the smaller disks will be used for the tops. Allow the filling to cool and, as it does, roll the dough for the shells and line the pans, letting the dough hang over the edge. Refrigerate for 20 minutes, fill them, then roll and attach the tops. Bake for 40 to 45 minutes.

Another option, of course, is to bake this in a single large, deep-dish pie pan or other similar-size casserole. Don't divide up the dough when you make it; just form it into a single disk. Roll it to size, then drape it over the filling and bake as directed.

MEATBALL POT PIE
WITH POLENTA TOPPING

This simple, satisfying pot pie was designed with convenience items in mind—namely, frozen packaged meatballs, pre-made polenta in a tube, and jarred tomato sauce. All you have to do is make the pastry and get it into the pan. (But by all means, if you're dying to make this from scratch, see the Recipe for Success.) I don't even bother to prebake the shells: Just spoon in the meatballs, top with the polenta and cheese, and away you go. Delish? You bet it is—a tasty hybrid between a childhood fantasy dish and sophisticated Italian cuisine. **Makes 4 servings**

1 recipe Go-To Pie Dough (page 22), divided as instructed in step 1 and refrigerated

FILLING

4 cups frozen fully cooked bite-size meatballs (no need to thaw)

1½ to 2 cups favorite tomato sauce

2 cups grated mozzarella cheese

1 (18-ounce) tube polenta

⅓ cup grated Parmesan cheese

Olive oil, for drizzling

1   Prepare the dough as instructed, dividing it into four equal balls. Flatten each ball into a disk, then wrap the disks individually in plastic wrap and refrigerate for at least 1½ hours. While the dough chills, get out four individual pie pans, each with a capacity of 1 to 1¼ cups.

2   Working with one piece of dough at a time (and leaving the others in the refrigerator), roll the dough into a 7½- to 8-inch circle on a lightly floured sheet of wax paper. The exact size will depend on your pie pans. Transfer the dough to the pan and press it in gently, taking care not to tear the dough. Roll and pinch the overhang of the dough into an upstanding ridge. Flute or crimp as desired. Refrigerate. Repeat for the other pans, refrigerating those as well.

3   Put the meatballs in a large skillet with about ⅛ inch of water. Cover and steam-thaw over medium heat for several minutes, just until the meatballs are warm inside. Drain the liquid from the pan or remove the lid and let what little bit of liquid there is simply evaporate. Remove from the heat. Using a butter knife (so you don't damage the pan), cut most of the meatballs in half and a few into quarters. This will help make the tops of the pot pies a little more level. Stir in the tomato sauce. Set aside.

4   Sprinkle 2 to 3 tablespoons mozzarella cheese in each pie shell. Divide the meatballs equally among all four pie shells. Using a fork, turn the upper layer of meatballs so their flat surfaces face up.

5   Using a serrated knife, cut thick slices of polenta—nearly ½ inch thick—and cover the top of the meatballs with them. (You won't need the entire tube.) You want a nice full, even layer; I find that you can get better coverage if you cut the polenta rounds into large triangles and then fit them close together on top. Sprinkle a generous tablespoon of Parmesan cheese over each one, then drizzle them with a little olive oil.

6   Place the pie pans on a large baking sheet and bake on the center rack for 35 minutes. Slide them out, cover each with an equal portion of the remaining mozzarella cheese, and continue to bake just until the cheese is good and melty, about 10 minutes more. Transfer to a rack and cool for 10 minutes before serving.

Recipe for Success

Of course, feel free to substitute your own small meatballs for the frozen ones. The ones I (occasionally) buy are about 1 inch in diameter. Same for the polenta: If you have some firm, homemade polenta in the fridge, by all means use it.

You don't need to be too compulsive about arranging the polenta on top and making a perfect surface, but if you're like me you'll probably find yourself cutting little shapes to fill in gaps and trying to make it look jigsaw-puzzle perfect, in spite of what I say.

SLOPPY JOE POT PIES
WITH A BISCUIT CRUST

This is something of a cooking project, and one where kids will enjoy pitching in with the assembly. It's pretty basic: Our good buttermilk biscuit dough is pressed into large muffin cups, then filled with homemade sloppy Joe filling and baked. Easy-peasy. You wind up with a crispy biscuit crust with lots of good saucy beef in the middle. Serve these with coleslaw or salad for a sleepover party, at tailgate parties, or during a football game down in the man cave. **Makes 6 servings**

1 recipe Tender Buttermilk Biscuit Crust (page 35), divided as instructed in step 1 and refrigerated

FILLING

2 tablespoons olive oil

½ large onion, finely chopped

½ green or red bell pepper, finely chopped

1 pound ground chuck

2 garlic cloves, minced

1 (15-ounce) can diced tomatoes, with their juice

½ cup ketchup or Heinz chili sauce

¼ cup barbecue sauce

1½ tablespoons light brown sugar

1 tablespoon yellow mustard

1 teaspoon chili powder

1 teaspoon Worcestershire sauce, plus more to taste

1½ cups grated cheddar or Monterey Jack cheese

1   Line a small baking sheet with a piece of plastic wrap. Dust it with flour. Prepare the biscuit dough, dividing it into six equal pieces. Using floured hands, shape the dough pieces into balls and place on the sheet. Gently flatten into disks about ½ inch thick, wrap, and refrigerate while you make the sloppy Joe filling.

2   Heat the olive oil in a large skillet, preferably nonstick, over medium heat. Add the onion and bell pepper. Sauté the vegetables for 7 minutes, then stir in the chuck and garlic. Brown the meat, breaking it up with a wooden spoon.

3   Add the tomatoes with their juice, ketchup, barbecue sauce, brown sugar, mustard, and chili powder to the meat. Stir in 1¼ cups water, the Worcestershire sauce, ½ teaspoon salt, and ground black pepper to taste. Bring the mixture to a simmer, and simmer gently until the meat is coated with plenty of full-bodied sauce, 10 to 15 minutes. Remove from the heat and cool for 15 minutes. Taste and correct the seasoning as needed.

4   While the meat cools, preheat the oven to 375°F. Get out and butter a 6-cup jumbo muffin pan. Lacking one, use ramekins or other small ovensafe dishes.

Recipe for Success

If you line the buttered muffin cups with thin strips of wax paper—about ½ inch wide and 8 inches long—leaving little tabs up above the top of the cups, you can lift up on the tabs for easy removal of the little pies.

5   Working with one piece of the biscuit dough at a time (and leaving the others in the refrigerator), flour your work surface and gently roll or pat the dough into a circle 5 inches in diameter. Place the circle of dough in one of the cups and press it in evenly, until the edge of the dough is even with the top of the cup. Repeat for the remaining pieces of dough.

6   Divide the sloppy Joe filling evenly among the dough shells; you can fill them right to the top. Bake on the center oven rack for 20 minutes. Slide the shelf out and sprinkle an equal amount of the cheese over each one. Slide the shelf back in and continue to bake just long enough to melt the cheese, about 5 minutes more.

7   Transfer the pan to a cooling rack and cool for about 10 minutes. Slide a butter knife down the edge of each shell and carefully work the shell up out of the cup. Set the pies directly on the rack and cool for another few minutes before serving.

FRITOS CHILI POT PIE

In case you've never heard of the famous Fritos pie, here's the basic recipe: Open a small bag of Fritos, add a scoop of hot chili and a handful of grated cheese, and eat right from the bag. It's great casual grub, and a tailgate classic, but it lacks a certain refinement as table fare— refinement I wanted to impart without going all upscale or losing the dish's rustic patina. So what did I do? I turned it into a pot pie, of course, and added a velvety, queso-like cheese sauce that gets spooned over the Fritos topping just before serving. Yum! No bag required; just bring a hearty appetite because you're going to dig in with relish. **Makes 4 servings**

1 recipe Go-To Pie Dough (page 22) or Whole Wheat Pie Dough (page 26), divided as instructed in step 1 and refrigerated

FILLING AND SAUCE

4 cups favorite beef and bean chili, at room temperature

8 ounces grated sharp cheddar cheese

2 teaspoons cornstarch

1 (12-ounce) can evaporated milk

1 teaspoon fresh lemon juice

½ teaspoon Dijon mustard

A few drops of hot sauce (optional)

4 large handfuls Fritos corn chips (a medium-size bag)

Sour cream, for garnish

Pickled jalapeño pepper slices, for garnish (optional)

1 Prepare the dough as instructed, but divide it into four equal pieces. Shape each piece into a ball, then flatten the balls into disks about ½ inch thick. Wrap the disks individually in plastic wrap and refrigerate for 1½ to 2 hours. While the dough chills, get out four individual pie pans, each with a capacity of 1 to 1¼ cups.

2 Working with one piece of dough at a time (and leaving the others in the refrigerator), roll the dough into a 7½- to 8-inch circle on a lightly floured sheet of wax paper. The exact size will depend on your pie pans. Transfer the dough to the pan and press it in gently, taking care not to tear the dough. Roll and pinch the overhang of the dough into an upstanding ridge. Flute or crimp as desired. Refrigerate. Repeat for the other pans, refrigerating those as well.

3 When you're ready to bake, preheat the oven to 375°F. Put a large, heavy baking sheet on one of the lower oven shelves to preheat at the same time. Spoon enough chili into each shell to come to within ½ inch of the rim. Place on the baking sheet in the oven and bake until the exposed edge of the crust is golden brown, about 35 minutes.

4   While the pies bake, make the cheese sauce. Combine the cheddar cheese and cornstarch in a medium-size saucepan, preferably nonstick. Add 1 cup of the evaporated milk. Begin cooking over medium heat, stirring almost nonstop. Continue to cook until the sauce is thickish and bubbly, about 5 minutes, adding more milk if necessary to thin it. Stir in the lemon juice, mustard, and, if you like, hot sauce. Remove from the heat.

5   When the pies are done, slide them out of the oven and transfer to a rack. Cool for 5 to 10 minutes, so they're not boiling hot, then top each one with a generous handful of Fritos. Reheat the sauce, adding a bit more liquid if necessary to correct the consistency—it should be like full-bodied queso—then ladle a generous scoop over the chips. Serve right away, passing the sour cream and, if you like, the pickled jalapeños at the table.

Recipe for Success

You can streamline this recipe, if you want, by skipping the cheese sauce. Top the Fritos with a handful of cheddar cheese, then return the pies to the oven until the cheese has melted. Still good, but I like the cheese sauce version more.

MOROCCAN LAMB PIE

This pot pie recipe is loosely based on Moroccan lamb stew, as well as a Todd English recipe I'm fond of. Meaty and saucy, it's got a bright, festive flavor, thanks to the assortment of sweet and aromatic seasonings. Don't be put off by the long list of ingredients. Many of them are herbs and spices, and you'll love the way they smell up the kitchen. **Makes 4 to 6 servings**

1 recipe Go-To Pie Dough (page 22), divided as instructed in step 1 and refrigerated

FILLING

3 to 4 tablespoons olive oil or vegetable oil

12 ounces lamb stew meat, cut in bite-size pieces

1 large onion, chopped

2 carrots, peeled and cut in small dice

2 celery ribs, finely chopped

1 small rutabaga, peeled and cut in ¼-inch dice

1 small russet potato, peeled and cut in ¼-inch dice

2 garlic cloves, minced

1 teaspoon curry powder

½ teaspoon ground cumin

¼ teaspoon ground allspice

¼ teaspoon ground ginger

¼ teaspoon crushed fennel seeds

1 cup dry red wine

2½ cups beef broth

1 cup rinsed and drained canned chickpeas

1 teaspoon chopped fresh rosemary

1 bay leaf

2½ tablespoons unsalted butter, at room temperature

2½ tablespoons all-purpose flour

1 to 2 teaspoons tomato paste (optional)

1 egg yolk beaten with 1 tablespoon milk

1   Prepare the dough as instructed, dividing it into four to six pieces, depending on the size of the individual pot pie pans you'll be using (they should each have a capacity of 1 to 1¼ cups). The pastry will be used for the top crust only—there is no bottom crust—so unless your pans are more than, say, 5 inches wide, you can probably get six out of a single batch of dough. Wrap each piece of dough in plastic wrap and refrigerate for at least 1½ hours.

2   Heat 2 tablespoons of the oil in a large stovetop casserole over medium heat. Add the lamb and brown the meat, stirring occasionally, for 4 minutes. Transfer the lamb to a bowl. Add another tablespoon or two of oil to the pan. Stir in the onion, carrots, and celery; salt lightly. Sweat the vegetables for 5 minutes, keeping them covered much of the time to trap the moisture. Stir in the rutabaga, potato, garlic, and spices. Cook for 1 minute, stirring often, then add the wine and bring to a low boil. Add the beef broth, chickpeas, rosemary, and bay leaf. Return the lamb to the pan and bring the stew to a simmer. Reduce the heat to low, cover, and simmer gently for 10 minutes.

3   Taste, adding salt and pepper as required; you'll likely need at least ¼ teaspoon salt, depending on the saltiness of your beef broth. Simmer, covered, for 10 more minutes.

4 Combine the softened butter and flour in a small bowl, mixing well with a spoon. Uncover the pot and continue to cook for 10 minutes more, gradually stirring in spoonfuls of the butter-flour mixture to thicken the filling. It should be very saucy and full bodied. Taste, and stir in a teaspoon or so of tomato paste, if you like, to sweeten the sauce. Set aside to cool.

5 When you're ready to bake, preheat the oven to 375°F. Put a large baking sheet on the center oven rack to preheat along with the oven. Butter your individual pot pie pans.

6 Divide the filling evenly among the buttered pans. Working with one piece of dough at a time (and leaving the others in the refrigerator), roll it out about 1 inch larger than the diameter of your pan. Drape the dough over the filling and pan, letting it hang down the sides. Using a paring knife, make a small steam vent in the pastry. Repeat for the rest of the pies. Lightly brush the pastry with the egg wash. Place the pies on the baking sheet in the oven and bake until the top crust is golden brown, about 35 minutes. Transfer the pies to a cooling rack and cool for about 10 minutes before serving.

Recipe for Success

A small handful of raisins (say, ¼ cup) would be right at home in these pies, so add them if that sounds good. Just stir them right in when you're adding the butter-flour thickener at the end. Also, if you have a small amount of diced canned tomatoes lurking in the fridge, maybe ¼ to ½ cup, you could add those near the end, instead of the tomato paste.

SHEPHERD'S PIES & A MEAT PIE MISCELLANY

TEX-MEX CHICKEN TORTILLA PIE

This is, admittedly, a pie only in the loosest sense of the word, but I'm fond enough of the dish that I have no reservations about including it; you won't doubt why it is here, either, once you've tried it. Our "crust" isn't a pastry or biscuit dough—it's softened corn tortilla wedges, arranged in a pie dish and then layered with salsa-seasoned chicken, corn, and a ricotta-cheddar cheese mixture. More tortilla pieces are layered between everything to help give the pie a firm texture that slices up nicely, just as a pie should. The flavor is out of this world—think Mexican-style lasagna—and you won't have any problem selling this to finicky family members. Go with an iceberg lettuce salad on the side, with creamy ranch dressing. **Makes 8 servings**

9 or 10 soft corn tortillas (5½ to 6 inches in diameter)

3½ tablespoons vegetable oil

1 large onion, finely chopped

2 garlic cloves, minced

2 cups chopped cooked chicken

2 teaspoons chili powder

1 teaspoon ground cumin

½ teaspoon smoked paprika

1 (16-ounce) jar favorite salsa

1 (15-ounce) container ricotta cheese

2½ cups grated sharp cheddar, Monterey Jack, or pepper Jack cheese

1 cup frozen corn kernels, thawed

1 (4-ounce) can chopped green chiles, drained

1   Get out a 9½-inch deep-dish pie pan and butter it lightly. Put one of your tortillas on a cutting board and cut it into a large wedge shape that's about 4 inches wide at the widest point and comes to a point along the opposite side of the tortilla. Place the wedge in your pan and see how it fits: The wide part should more or less come up to the top edge and the point should be in or near the center. If you like the fit, cut eight more of them—just lay the first one on top of a stack, then cut. Keep the trimmings, because you'll need them.

2   Heat 1½ tablespoons of the oil in a large skillet over medium heat. Holding one of the tortilla wedges with tongs, warm the wedge in the hot oil for no more than 2 or 3 seconds on each side. Don't even let go with your tongs; it's that quick. Position the wedge in the pan as you did earlier, pressing it in snugly. Repeat for the remaining wedges, butting them up against one another to form a pie shell. Heat one whole tortilla and lay it in the bottom center, on top of the others. Set aside.

3   Add the remaining 2 tablespoons oil to the same skillet and heat over medium heat. Stir in the onion and sauté for 5 to 6 minutes. Stir in the garlic, chicken, chili powder, cumin, and smoked paprika. Stir for another 30 seconds, then add the salsa. Bring to a simmer, adding salt and pepper to taste. The sauce mixture should not be too thick, because the tortilla layers absorb a lot of liquid, so thin it with a little water, if necessary. Remove from the heat. Preheat the oven to 375°F.

4   In a medium mixing bowl, combine the ricotta cheese and 2 cups of the cheddar. Mix gently with a fork, adding salt and pepper to taste. Set aside. Sprinkle the remaining ½ cup cheddar in the pie shell.

5   To assemble the pie, spoon half of the chicken mixture into the shell. Smooth it out, then cover it with a loose single layer of tortilla trimmings, using about half of them. Top the trimmings with all of the corn and the chiles, spreading them evenly. Dollop half of the ricotta mixture here and there over that. Cover the cheese with another loose layer of tortilla trimmings. Top them with the remaining chicken mixture, then the rest of the ricotta mixture.

6   Cover the pie with foil, tented up so it doesn't press against the cheese. Bake for 45 minutes on the center oven rack, then remove the foil and continue to bake for 5 to 10 minutes more. Don't be surprised if the filling doesn't juice up and bubble; as I said, the tortillas will absorb much of the liquid. Transfer to a rack and cool for at least 20 minutes before serving.

Recipe for Success

Just so it's clear, the whole point of heating the tortilla wedges in oil is to make them good and flexible, so they contour to the pan and fit well. The oil also helps the tortillas turn crispy-crunchy as the pie bakes; the crust would be flabby without it.

AMERICAN CHEESEBURGER PIE

As the name implies, this one will remind you of eating a good old American cheeseburger. There's nothing subtle about it, nor is there meant to be: It's just great, in-your-face—or should I say, in-your-mouth—beef flavor, highlighted by the seasonings we love with our burgers: Worcestershire sauce, chili sauce or ketchup, and pickles. A top layer of tomatoes helps keep the meat moist, and the cheese goes on right at the end so it stays melty good. I like the biscuit crust here better than a flaky pastry because it's more porous and absorbs lots of flavor. **Makes 8 servings**

1 recipe Cornmeal Biscuit Crust (page 34), prepared as described in step 1 and refrigerated

FILLING

1 tablespoon vegetable oil

4 slices bacon, chopped

1½ pounds ground chuck

½ large onion, finely chopped

2 garlic cloves, minced

⅓ cup dry Italian-style bread crumbs

2 large eggs

⅓ cup whole milk

3 tablespoons Heinz chili sauce

1½ tablespoons Dijon or yellow mustard

1 tablespoon Worcestershire sauce

¼ cup dill or sweet pickle relish

2½ cups grated sharp or extra-sharp cheddar cheese

2 medium tomatoes, cored, seeded, and thinly sliced

1   If you haven't already, prepare and refrigerate the biscuit dough. Unless you like a pretty thick crust, I recommend that you don't use quite all of this dough to line your pan. So before shaping your dough disk, I would cut off and set aside enough dough to make about four individual biscuits. (You can shape and then bake them while this pie bakes. Or freeze them for later.)

2   Butter a 9½-inch deep-dish pie pan. Flour your chilled dough and roll it into a 12-inch circle on a well-floured work surface or floured parchment paper, taking care that it doesn't stick. Drape the dough in the pan, then tuck it in gently so you can see the crease around the perimeter of the bottom. Pinch the top edge of the dough into an even ridge. Refrigerate while you make the filling.

3   Heat the oil in a very large skillet over medium heat and add the bacon. When it has rendered some fat, add the chuck and onion. Brown the meat thoroughly, breaking it up with a wooden spoon. Stir in the garlic when the meat is almost done.

4   Remove the pan from the heat, tilt it, and spoon off and discard about two-thirds of the fat. Transfer the meat and remaining fat to a large mixing bowl. Add the bread crumbs, ¾ teaspoon salt, and ¼ teaspoon ground black pepper. Mix well.

5   Whisk together the eggs, milk, chili sauce, mustard, and Worcestershire sauce in another large bowl. Add to the meat along with the pickle relish and 1 cup of the cheese. Mix well. Set aside for 15 minutes while you preheat the oven to 375°F.

6   Spread the meat mixture evenly in the refrigerated pie shell. Top with a single layer of tomatoes. Bake on the center oven rack for 30 minutes. Slide the pie out and top with the remaining 1½ cups cheddar. Continue to bake for 10 minutes more. Transfer to a rack and cool for at least 15 minutes before serving.

Recipe for Success

You'll notice that I seeded the tomatoes that get layered on top of the pie. They'll still be good and juicy even without the seeds, and you'll avoid leaving a less-than-appetizing excess of tomato juice on top of the pie.

ITALIAN SAUSAGE & CHICKEN SKILLET PIE

Sometimes I'll have a pastry all made up and waiting in the fridge with no particular use for it in mind. When that happens, I've been known to start tossing things in a skillet—meats, veggies, maybe some leftover beans, and perhaps some broth, gravy, or sauce—hoping that the concoction turns out well enough to warrant a top crust. I call these creations "skillet pies" and, on occasion, they're so good that I retrace my steps and get it down on paper. This is one such pie, a sort of heady Italian stew that practically begged to be crusted. Skillet pies aren't fancy; you leave the filling right in the skillet, top with the pastry, and bake. But they sure are good. **Makes 6 servings**

1 recipe Go-To Pie Dough (page 22), refrigerated

FILLING

3 hot or mild Italian sausages (about 12 ounces total)

3 tablespoons olive oil

1 large onion, chopped

1 medium green or red bell pepper, seeded and chopped

1 pound boneless, skinless chicken breast or thighs, cut into bite-size chunks

3 garlic cloves, minced

2½ tablespoons all-purpose flour

2 cups diced canned tomatoes, with their juice

1¼ cups chicken broth

1 cup rinsed and drained canned chickpeas

1 teaspoon dried basil

1 teaspoon dried oregano

1 cup crumbled feta cheese, for garnish (optional)

1   If you haven't already, prepare the pastry and refrigerate it for at least 1½ hours.

2   Pour several inches of water into a medium-size saucepan. Bring to a boil over medium-high heat. Poke the sausages several times with a paring knife or fork and add to the water. Boil for 5 minutes, then remove from the heat. (They won't be fully cooked at this point, so don't sample them.) Transfer to a plate and set aside.

3   Heat the oil in a deep, 10- to 11-inch ovensafe skillet over medium heat. Add the onion and bell pepper. Sauté the vegetables for 3 to 4 minutes, then stir in the chicken. Cut the sausages into ½-inch pieces and add them as well. Sauté for 3 to 4 minutes more, then stir in the garlic and flour. Cook, stirring, for 1 minute, then stir in the tomatoes with their juice, chicken broth, chickpeas, basil, and oregano. Bring to a simmer, then cover and simmer gently for 10 minutes, stirring occasionally. Taste, adding salt and pepper as necessary. Remove from the heat and set aside to cool. Preheat the oven to 375°F.

4   On a floured work surface, roll the pastry into a circle a little larger than the diameter of the skillet. Drape it over the filling, tucking the excess down into the filling. Poke one or two steam vents in the middle of the pastry with a paring knife.

5   Bake the pie on the center oven rack until the pastry is golden brown and the filling is bubbly, about 40 minutes. Transfer to a rack and cool for 10 to 15 minutes before serving. Pass the feta cheese at the table, if you like.

Recipe for Success

In case you don't have an oven-safe skillet, you'll need to transfer the filling to an oiled baking dish before it goes in the oven. Something medium-ish will work best. If you like more crust, choose something a little bigger. If you like a thicker filling, go smaller.

For a nice touch, mix the feta cheese with a few tablespoons chopped fresh flat-leaf parsley. This makes for a good-looking garnish, and the parsley really brightens up the flavor.

TOURTIÈRE, MY WAY

Tourtière is the traditional double crusted French Canadian meat pie, versions of which are also found throughout much of northern New England. Unlike our saucy pot pies, tourtière recipes are typically much more dense and compact—not quite like meatloaf, but almost. Because tourtière is typically served during the holidays, seasonings such as cloves and cinnamon often appear in recipes, but—to be perfectly frank, and with apologies to my neighbors up north—I often find them underwhelming, seasoning-wise. That's how the Worcestershire sauce and ketchup ended up in here. I'd feel more guilty about these Americanizations were it not for the fact that no two of the dozens of tourtière recipes I've seen can quite agree on how it should be made. I rest my case. P.S. This is a great company dish. It just needs a salad on the side. **Makes 8 to 10 servings**

1 recipe Go-To Pie Dough for a Double Crust (page 24) or Cheddar Cheese Pastry (page 32), refrigerated

FILLING

2 tablespoons vegetable oil

1 large onion, chopped

4 garlic cloves, minced

2 cups chopped white mushroom caps

1 pound ground pork

1 pound ground beef

2 cups beef broth

1 large baking potato, peeled and cut into small dice

1 carrot, peeled and cut into small dice

1 bay leaf

1 teaspoon dried thyme

½ teaspoon chopped dried rosemary

½ teaspoon paprika

¼ teaspoon ground cinnamon

¼ teaspoon ground cloves

¼ cup ketchup

1 teaspoon Worcestershire sauce

3 tablespoons old-fashioned (not instant) rolled oats

1   If you haven't already, prepare and refrigerate the pastry for at least 1½ hours.

2   Heat the oil in a large stovetop casserole or Dutch oven over medium heat. Stir in the onion and sauté for 5 minutes. Stir in the garlic and mushrooms; salt lightly. Sauté for 2 to 3 minutes more, then add the meats, crumbling them up as they go in the pan. Brown the meat, breaking it up with a wooden spoon. Remove the pot from the heat, tilt it, and spoon off and discard all but 2 to 3 tablespoons of the fat in the pan.

3   Put the pot back on the heat and stir in the beef broth, potato, carrot, bay leaf, thyme, rosemary, paprika, cinnamon, cloves, ¾ teaspoon salt, and ¼ teaspoon ground black pepper. Bring to a low boil, then lower the heat, cover, and simmer for 20 to 25 minutes.

4   When the potatoes are good and soft, stir in the ketchup, Worcestershire sauce, and oats. Take a potato masher and mash the mixture to break up the potatoes a bit; the liquid in the pan will start to thicken pretty quickly. Continue to simmer the mixture over medium heat, stirring often, until it's thick but still a little saucy. Transfer the filling to a shallow casserole, remove the bay leaf, and cool thoroughly.

5   While the filling cools, roll the larger half of the pastry into a 13-inch circle on a floured work surface. Line a 9½-inch deep-dish pie pan with it, letting the edge of the pastry drape over the sides of the pan; don't trim it. Refrigerate until the filling has cooled.

6   When you're ready to assemble the pie, preheat the oven to 375°F and adjust the oven rack so it is one position below center. Transfer the cooled filling to the pie shell and level it out with a spoon. Moisten the edge of the pastry with a wet pastry brush.

7   Roll the other half of the pastry into an 11-inch circle on a floured work surface and drape it over the filling. Press along the perimeter to seal, then sculpt the excess dough into an upstanding ridge. Flute or crimp with a fork as desired.

8   Bake the pie for 30 minutes, then move the oven rack and pie up to the center position and continue to bake until the crust is a rich golden brown, 15 to 20 minutes more. Cool on a rack for at least 20 minutes before slicing and serving. If you can let it sit even longer, that's better, because the filling will become more solid.

Recipe for Success

I like the oats in this meat pie. It's not a common ingredient in this dish, but—like the mushrooms I've included—they show up from time to time, no doubt to help stretch the filling and make it a little more compact. I've seen a number of recipes that had far more oats than I use here. Don't worry that they'll intrude in the finished pie; they more or less disappear the way oats (or bread crumbs) do in a meatloaf.

Do sample the filling when you transfer it to the casserole to cool. You may want to kick up the seasoning even more, adding additional ketchup, Worcestershire, spices, or rosemary to suit your taste.

TARTE CHOUCROUTE

Whoever decided that *choucroute garnie*—the classic French dish of sauerkraut and sausage—could be reimagined as a savory pastry is my kind of cook. If the thought of a sauerkraut dinner pie doesn't exactly ring your bell, I suggest withholding judgment and making this dish at your first opportunity. It is, in a word, excellent—layers of sauerkraut, sautéed onion, and sausage topped with a sour cream custard heavily laced with mustard. **Makes 8 servings**

1 recipe Go-To Pie Dough (page 22), refrigerated

FILLING

6 slices thick bacon, cut into ½-inch pieces

1 large onion, halved and thinly sliced

1 pound sauerkraut, drained in a colander

¼ teaspoon caraway seeds, crushed (optional)

3 large eggs

1⅓ cups sour cream

⅓ cup whole milk or half-and-half

1 tablespoon Dijon mustard

2 teaspoons all-purpose flour

1½ cups grated Swiss or Gruyère cheese

6 ounces fully cooked bratwursts or kielbasa, cut into bite-size pieces

1   If you haven't already, prepare the pastry and refrigerate it for at least 1½ to 2 hours.

2   On a lightly floured sheet of wax paper, roll the dough into a 13- to 13½-inch circle. Invert the pastry over a 9½- to 10-inch tart pan, center it, then peel off the paper. Gently tuck the pastry into the pan without stretching it, and sculpt the edge into an upstanding ridge. Refrigerate the shell for 1 hour, then partially prebake and cool according to the directions on page 18. Preheat the oven to 375°F.

3   Heat a large skillet over medium heat and add the bacon. Cook until crisp. Transfer to a plate, leaving about 3 tablespoons of bacon fat in the pan. Stir in the onion and cook until light golden, about 12 minutes. While it cooks, use your hands to squeeze much of the liquid out of the sauerkraut (see page 54) and set it aside. When the onion is ready, stir in the sauerkraut and, if you like, the caraway seeds. Remove from the heat.

4   In a large bowl, whisk the eggs until blended. Whisk in the sour cream, milk, mustard, flour, ¾ teaspoon salt, and ground black pepper to taste. Stir in the cheese.

5   To assemble the tart, spread the sausage in the shell and spoon the onion and sauerkraut mixture over it, making it as level as possible. Pour the custard evenly over the sauerkraut; smooth with a spoon. Crumble the bacon and spread it over the top.

6   Bake the tart on the center oven rack until the top is puffed and browned somewhat and there is no evidence of uncooked custard in the center, 40 to 45 minutes. Transfer to a rack and cool for at least 30 minutes before serving.

> **Recipe for Success**
>
> If you're watching your intake of meat, you can always leave out the sausage. It's not quite the same, but it's still darn good, with a robust bacon flavor.

SHEPHERD'S PIE

Some day, when you're good and bored, go online and Google this: *Should shepherd's pie have a pastry or not?* You'll be shocked at how many unpleasantries this question provokes. (At least, I was.) You'll find threads of conversations, some going back years, with one party or another tossing the gravest of insults back and forth, cursing not just the offender but also the offender's ancestors and any future progeny. It's like shepherd's pie road rage, just without the road. I cringe to think what might come my way when someone discovers that I often put a pastry under my shepherd's pie. I'll let the chips fall where they may because this version—with a flaky bottom crust, a meaty filling, and a crown of sour creamed mashed potatoes—tastes positively glorious. It's best to make this recipe in individual dishes to maintain the integrity of the construction. And in the end, if you want to dispense with the pastry, this is wonderful even without. **Makes 4 servings**

1 recipe Go-To Pie Dough (page 22), divided as instructed in step 1 and refrigerated

FILLING

2 tablespoons vegetable oil

1 large onion, chopped

1 large carrot, peeled and cut in small dice

2 celery ribs, finely chopped

1½ pounds ground chuck

2 garlic cloves, minced

2½ tablespoons all-purpose flour

½ teaspoon paprika

1½ cups beef broth

1 cup canned diced tomatoes, with their juice

1 cup frozen peas or baby lima beans (no need to thaw)

1 tablespoon tomato paste

1 teaspoon Worcestershire sauce

1 teaspoon brown sugar

½ teaspoon chopped fresh rosemary

½ teaspoon dried thyme

MASHED POTATO TOPPING

6 cups peeled and coarsely chopped russet potatoes

5 tablespoons unsalted butter, melted

¼ cup sour cream

⅓ to ½ cup warm whole milk

1   Prepare the pastry, dividing it into four equal pieces rather than one disk. Flatten each piece into a ½-inch-thick disk, then wrap the disks individually in plastic wrap. Refrigerate for at least 1½ hours.

2   Get out four individual pie pans, each with a capacity of 1 to 1¼ cups. Working with one piece of dough at a time (and leaving the others in the refrigerator), roll the dough into a circle 7½ to 8 inches in diameter. Line one of the pans with the pastry; shape and flute the edge. Refrigerate. Repeat for the other pie pans, refrigerating those as well.

3   Heat the oil in a large stovetop casserole over medium heat. Add the onion, carrot, and celery; salt lightly. Cover the pan and sweat the vegetables for 5 minutes, stirring occasionally. Add the ground chuck and garlic. Brown the meat, breaking it up with a wooden spoon. When the meat is browned, remove the pan from the heat. Tilt the pan and spoon off and discard about two-thirds of the fat.

Continued

4 Put the pan back on the heat and stir in the flour and paprika. Cook for 1 minute, then add the beef broth, tomatoes and their juice, and the peas. Bring to a simmer, then stir in the tomato paste, Worcestershire sauce, brown sugar, rosemary, thyme, ½ teaspoon salt, and ¼ teaspoon ground black pepper. Simmer the filling gently until thick and saucy, 5 to 7 minutes. Taste, adding more seasoning as needed. Remove from the heat and cool to room temperature (see Recipe for Success).

5 Plan to start making the mashed potato topping shortly before the pies will go in the oven. You'll start baking the pies without the potatoes and then add them about halfway through the baking. Put the potatoes in a large saucepan with enough lightly salted water to cover. Bring to a boil over medium-high heat, then reduce the heat and cook at a low boil until tender, 10 to 12 minutes. Drain. (Reserve the potato water for soup, if you like.) Transfer the potatoes to a large mixing bowl. Add 3 tablespoons of the butter, the sour cream, and about ¼ cup of the warm milk. Mash with a hand masher, adding salt and pepper to taste. Use more milk as needed to make the potatoes fluffy-moist but not too soft or loose. Cover the bowl with plastic wrap to keep the potatoes warm. Preheat the oven to 375°F. Put a large, heavy baking sheet on the center oven rack to preheat along with the oven.

6 Spoon enough filling into each pie shell to come within ½ inch of the top of the shell. (Don't be surprised if you have extra filling—see Recipe for Success.) Place the pie pans on the baking sheet and bake for 25 minutes. Slide out the baking sheet and put it on a heatproof surface. Mound lots of mashed potatoes on top of the filling, smoothing it with the back of a spoon. Brush the surface of the potatoes with the last 2 tablespoons melted butter.

7 Bake the pies for 20 minutes more. Transfer the pies to a cooling rack and cool for at least 15 minutes before serving.

Recipe for Success

It's important to cool the meat filling before it goes into the shells. If you put hot filling into the shells, much of the moisture in the sauce is going to evaporate before the pastry has time to bake, leaving you with dry filling. If there's time, I actually prefer to cool and then refrigerate the meat, so both it and the pastry are cold when the pies start baking.

If you do have leftover filling and mashed potatoes, just make up crustless versions of the pies and refrigerate or freeze them for later.

I'll sometimes cover the mashed potatoes with cheese right after coating them with butter. My favorites are grated Parmesan or sharp cheddar.

SWEET POTATO SHEPHERD'S PIE

Here's a shepherd's pie recipe for the adventurous cook, a spicy-saucy meat filling topped with tangy mashed sweet potatoes, all in a flaky pastry. I always make this recipe as individual pies, though I can't imagine it wouldn't work just fine as one larger pie in a deep-dish pie pan. As with shepherd's pies generally, you want to be sure that you end up with a good amount of sauce with the meat, so don't reduce the sauce too much on the stovetop prior to filling your pie shells. What this lacks in tradition, it makes up for in great taste and good looks. **Makes 4 servings**

1 recipe Go-To Pie Dough (page 22), divided as instructed in step 1 and refrigerated

FILLING AND SWEET POTATO TOPPING

3 medium-large sweet potatoes, scrubbed

3 tablespoons unsalted butter, at room temperature

3 tablespoons sour cream

1 to 2 teaspoons sugar

2 tablespoons olive oil

1 large onion, chopped

1 carrot, peeled and diced

1½ cups chopped white mushroom caps

8 ounces ground chuck

8 ounces hot or mild Italian sausage meat, out of the casing

2 tablespoons all-purpose flour

½ teaspoon paprika

2 cups beef broth

½ cup dry red wine

2 tablespoons tomato paste

1 cup frozen green beans (no need to thaw)

1   Prepare the pastry as instructed, but divide it into four equal-size balls. Press each ball into a disk about ½ inch thick. Wrap the balls individually in plastic wrap and refrigerate them for 1½ to 2 hours.

2   Get out four individual pie pans, each with a capacity of 1 to 1¼ cups. Working with one ball of dough at a time (and leaving the others in the refrigerator), roll it into a circle 7½ to 8 inches in diameter. Line one of the pans with it, rolling and sculpting the overhang into an upstanding ridge. Refrigerate, then repeat for the remaining balls of dough.

3   Preheat the oven to 400°F. Poke each of the sweet potatoes several times with a paring knife. Place them on a foil-lined baking sheet and bake until tender in the middle when pierced with a toothpick or skewer, 50 minutes to 1 hour. Set aside to cool.

4   When the potatoes have cooled just enough to handle, scoop out the warm flesh and transfer it to a mixing bowl. Add the butter, sour cream, sugar, and ¼ teaspoon salt. Using a potato masher, mash the potatoes until smooth, but don't overdo it. Taste and add more salt as needed. Set aside.

5   Heat the olive oil in a large skillet over medium heat. Stir in the onion, carrot, and mushrooms and sauté for 3 to 4 minutes. Add the meats and brown them, breaking them up with a wooden spoon; salt and pepper to taste. Add the flour and paprika and cook, stirring, for 30 seconds. Stir in the broth and red wine. Bring to a simmer, then stir in the tomato paste.

6   Simmer the mixture for 5 to 10 minutes, then add the green beans. Continue to simmer the mixture until it is thick but still quite saucy, another 5 minutes or so. Remove from the heat and set aside to cool.

7   When you're ready to bake the pot pies, preheat the oven to 375°F. Put a large baking sheet on the center oven rack to preheat. Divide the meat mixture evenly among the chilled pie shells. Top each one with an equal portion of the mashed sweet potatoes, smoothing the tops with the back of a spoon. Put the pot pies on the baking sheet in the oven and bake until you can see the sauce start to bubble up from below, about 40 minutes. Transfer to a rack and cool for at least 10 minutes before serving.

Recipe for Success

Whenever you have a hot filling, as we do here, let it cool before adding it to your chilled shells. Otherwise, you risk melting the fat in the pastry and making it less flaky. To cool a filling quicker, transfer it out of the pan you cooked it in and into another container.

AUSSIE MEAT PIES

Whether it's great American classics or recipes I'm not all that familiar with, I enjoy scouring the Internet for new recipes, comparing similar ones side by side, test driving a few, and then melding their best features to come up with something original. That's pretty much the history of this recipe. I approached the subject thinking that the formula for an "Aussie meat pie" was cast in stone, but that turned out to be no more valid than discovering one irrefutable recipe for American meatloaf: Variations abound. There *are* Aussie pie similarities: Ground beef seems to be the meat of choice. Beef broth and ketchup are frequent common denominators. A flour slurry is typically added to thicken the meat. And, of particular interest to pie makers, they often have a pie pastry bottom crust and puff pastry lid, which is the way I've done it here. In the end, I think I came up with a fairly authentic rendition that's suitably saucy-meaty and has the right blend of seasonings, and one you'll be proud to serve your family and friends. **Makes 6 pies**

1 recipe Flaky and Sturdy Hand Pie Pastry (page 38), divided as instructed in step 1 and refrigerated

FILLING

1 tablespoon vegetable oil

2 slices bacon, cut in ½-inch pieces

1 large onion, chopped

2 pounds ground beef chuck

1½ cups beef broth

½ cup ketchup

2 tablespoons barbecue sauce

1 tablespoon Worcestershire sauce

1 teaspoon dried oregano

⅛ teaspoon ground nutmeg

2 tablespoons all-purpose flour

1 cup grated sharp cheddar cheese

1 sheet frozen puff pastry, thawed

1 egg yolk beaten with 1 tablespoon milk

1   Prepare the pastry as instructed, but divide it into six pieces instead of four. Flatten each piece into a ½-inch-thick disk. Wrap the disks individually in plastic wrap and refrigerate for at least 1½ hours.

2   Heat the oil in a very large skillet or stovetop casserole over medium heat, tilting the pan to spread the fat around. Add the bacon and cook until the bacon has rendered much of its fat and started to turn crisp. Add the onion and sauté for 5 minutes, stirring often.

3   Add the ground chuck to the pan. Brown the meat, breaking it up thoroughly with a wooden spoon. Stir in the beef broth, ketchup, barbecue sauce, Worcestershire sauce, oregano, nutmeg, and ¼ teaspoon each salt and ground black pepper. Bring to a simmer, then cover the pan and simmer gently for 20 minutes. Taste, adding more salt and pepper as needed.

4   Put the flour in a small bowl and whisk in about 2 tablespoons water, just enough to make a slurry. Add the slurry to the meat and stir well. Continue to simmer the meat mixture until it becomes thick and saucy, 3 to 4 minutes more. Remove from the heat and stir in the cheese. Transfer the mixture to a shallow baking dish and set aside to cool. Cover and refrigerate for 2 to 3 hours or overnight.

5   When you're ready to bake, preheat the oven to 375°F. Put a large baking sheet on the center oven rack to preheat along with the oven. Get out six individual pie pans, each with a capacity of ¾ to 1 cup. Working with one piece of dough at a time, roll it into a 6- to 6½-inch circle and line one of your pie pans with it. Using a paring knife, trim the overhang so it is flush with the rim of the pan. Refrigerate. Repeat for the remaining pieces of dough.

6   Moisten the filling with a tablespoon or so of water to loosen it; just work the water in with a spoon. Pack enough filling in each of the shells so it's more or less level with the rim and slightly mounded in the center. Using a round cutter, cut six circles of puff pastry about ¼ inch larger than the diameter of your pans. Moisten the outer edge of the shell with a wet fingertip. Lay a circle of puff pastry on top of the filling and press along the edge to seal. The edges of both pastries should pretty much line up. Repeat for the other pies. Brush each one with a little of the egg wash.

7   Place the pies on the baking sheet and bake for 15 minutes. Reduce the heat to 350°F and continue to bake until the tops are a rich golden brown, about 15 minutes more. Transfer the pies to a rack and cool for 10 to 15 minutes before serving.

Recipe for Success

It's very important to fully cool the filling before putting it in the shells, so don't skip this step. Yes, this lengthens the overall prep time for these pies, but consider making the meat filling—and the pie pastry—one day, and then assembling and baking these the next.

If you want to remove some of the fat from this dish, remove the pan from the heat after browning the beef, then tilt the pan and spoon off some of the fat.

These pies are a little smaller than some of the other individual pies in this collection. If your pans are a little larger than the ones called for, you can make four pies. Roll the bottom pastry to 7½ to 8 inches in diameter, and adjust the size of the puff pastry lids as necessary.

COBBLERS, STRUDELS & OTHER WRAPPED ENTRÉES

ROASTED VEGETABLE STRUDEL

This strudel was inspired by a sort of roasted ratatouille that I often make during the summer months to toss with cold pasta. Come to find out it also makes a great filling wrapped in pastry, strudel style. You'll probably have all these veggies on hand in your summer kitchen; add a small handful of fresh herbs and your choice of cheese to make this strudel your own. **Makes 4 to 6 servings**

1 recipe Go-To Pie Dough (page 22), prepared as instructed in step 1 and refrigerated

FILLING

1 medium eggplant, peeled and cut into ½-inch dice

1½ small to medium zucchini, cut into ½-inch dice

½ bell pepper (any color), chopped

4 or 5 plum tomatoes, cored and coarsely chopped but not seeded

1 medium onion, chopped

2 garlic cloves, minced

2 to 3 tablespoons chopped fresh Italian herbs, such as basil,

thyme, oregano, and rosemary, in whatever combination you like best

¼ cup olive oil, plus more for drizzling

1 to 1½ cups cheese (see Recipe for Success)

1 egg beaten with 1 tablespoon milk (optional)

1   Prepare the pastry as instructed, but instead of shaping it into a disk, shape it into a square about ¾ inch thick. Cover in plastic wrap and refrigerate for 1½ to 2 hours.

2   Preheat the oven to 425°F. Line two large rimmed baking sheets with parchment paper or aluminum foil. Oil lightly. Combine all of the vegetables and herbs in a large mixing bowl. Add the olive oil and toss with your hands. Salt and pepper the mixture generously and toss again. Spread the vegetables evenly on the baking sheets. Drizzle with a little more olive oil.

3   Roast the vegetables until crunchy-tender, about 30 minutes. You'll probably have to do this on two different oven shelves, so switch baking sheet positions about midway through so the vegetables cook evenly (you might give the vegetables a toss while you're at it). Transfer to racks and cool thoroughly.

4   When you're ready to bake the strudel, preheat the oven to 375°F. On a lightly floured sheet of parchment paper, roll the pastry into a 9 x 15-inch rectangle. (It's easier if you roll directly on the parchment paper so you can lift it onto your baking sheet and bake right on the parchment.)

5 Spread the vegetable filling in a 4-inch-wide row down one long side of the pastry, leaving a ½-inch border uncovered along the edges. Top with whatever cheese you're using, distributing it evenly over the vegetables. Moisten that edge with a wet fingertip. Fold the uncovered half of the pastry over the filling, lining up the edges. Press the edges to seal, then fold the edge under slightly to hide the seam. Lift the parchment and strudel onto the baking sheet. Using a serrated knife, make 3 or 4 diagonal slits in the top of the pastry. Lightly brush the strudel with the egg wash, if desired, for a darker, glossier finish.

6 Bake the strudel for about 40 minutes. When done, the strudel will look a little bit swollen and you will likely see some active juice through the slits. Transfer the pan to a cooling rack. Cool for at least 15 minutes before slicing and serving.

Recipe for Success

Unless you're using a giant, restaurant-style roasting pan, don't try to roast the vegetables in a single pan. If they're too crowded they'll just sort of stew, when what you're looking for is a bit of that roasted char flavor. Don't be surprised—just delighted—if this makes more filling than you can fit into your strudel. Any leftovers can be added to pasta, pasta sauce, or rice, or used to fill an omelet, among many other possible uses.

As for the cheeses, you have all sorts of options. I've used grated mozzarella alone or with some freshly grated Parmesan; or, for a little added moisture, try ½ cup ricotta mixed with 2 or 3 tablespoons pesto along with another cheese. You really can't miss.

SALMON & SPINACH PASTRY PACKETS

Fish in pastry isn't something you see much nowadays, and that's just enough of a shame that I hereby declare its imminent comeback. This recipe should help. You'll sauté some spinach, make a bed of it on your perfectly rolled pastry, dollop with savory cream cheese, and then place a generous salmon fillet on top. Seal and bake. With the addition of the pastry, cheese, and spinach, a typical one-serving portion of fish becomes two. These packets are fancy enough to be served at an intimate dinner, but easy enough to do for a regular weekend dinner, especially if you make the dough ahead. **Makes 4 servings**

1 recipe Go-To Pie Dough (page 22), divided as instructed in step 1 and refrigerated

FILLING

2 tablespoons unsalted butter

8 ounces baby spinach, coarsely chopped

2 garlic cloves, minced

4 ounces cream cheese, at room temperature

½ cup grated Parmesan cheese

1 to 2 teaspoons whole milk

2 (6½- to 7-ounce) boneless, skinless salmon fillets

Old Bay Seasoning or other seafood seasoning

1 egg beaten with 1 tablespoon milk (optional)

1   Prepare the pastry as directed, but divide the dough into two equal portions and shape each into a square almost ¾ inch thick. Wrap each square in plastic wrap and refrigerate for at least 1½ hours.

2   Melt the butter in a large sauté pan over medium heat. Stir in the spinach and garlic; salt lightly. Sauté for several minutes, until the spinach is thoroughly wilted. Remove from the heat and allow to cool.

3   In a small bowl, blend the cream cheese and Parmesan cheese; pepper to taste. Mix in a teaspoon or two of milk to soften further. Set aside. Preheat the oven to 375°F and line a large baking sheet with parchment paper.

4   Working with one piece of dough at a time (and leaving the other one in the refrigerator), roll it into a rectangle on a lightly floured sheet of parchment paper. It should be large enough that when you place half of the spinach, dolloped cheese, and salmon on one side of it, you'll have plenty of dough to fold over and cover the filling, plus enough left uncovered along the edges to seal. To accommodate the 1-inch-thick salmon fillets I get, my rectangle is usually about 7 inches by 10 or 11 inches.

5   Draw an imaginary line down the center of your pastry, widthwise, and make a bed of about half of the spinach, in the approximate dimensions of your salmon fillet, in the center of one side. Dollop about half of the cheese mixture here and there over the spinach. Sprinkle one piece of salmon on both sides with Old Bay and salt; go easy on the salt because many seafood seasoning mixes have plenty of it. Place the fillet on top of the cheese and press lightly to flatten it.

6   Lightly moisten the entire edge of the pastry with a wet fingertip. Fold the uncovered half of pastry snugly over the salmon. Line up the edges of the pastry, press them together gently, and roll them into a sort of rope edge to seal. Lift the parchment and fish packet onto the baking sheet. Repeat for the other portion of pastry and the remaining fillings.

7   Using a serrated knife, make a 3-inch-long shallow slit, lengthwise, in the top of each pastry. Brush with egg wash, if you like, and bake on the center oven rack for 35 to 40 minutes. It's a little tricky knowing exactly when the fish is done, because you can't fork it to see if it's flaky (at least not without making a mess of the pastry). However, an instant-read thermometer inserted into the thickest part of the fish should register 145°F. Use a spatula to transfer the packets to a cooling rack and cool for about 10 minutes. Halve widthwise and serve.

Recipe for Success

Fish fillets are often thicker here, thinner there, which can cause uneven cooking. If you feel confident enough to do a little salmon surgery, you can often remedy this simply by slicing some flesh away from the thickest area and laying it on top of the thinnest area. It doesn't have to look pretty, because everything is covered in pastry. And it will make the pocket look more squared away, so it's probably worth the small bit of trouble.

OLD-FASHIONED CHICKEN & BISCUITS

I love chicken and dumplings, but I love chicken and biscuits even more because you get a more pronounced textural contrast between the crusty biscuits and the saucy chicken underneath, the way a dinner pie should be. This is a down-home American classic, the sort of dish they would have served on farm tables at least once a week in the days of yore. One taste and you'll agree that it's a weekly tradition worth reviving. **Makes 6 servings**

1⅓ cups all-purpose flour

3½ pounds bone-in, skin-on split chicken breasts and thighs (legs are fine, too)

3 tablespoons olive oil

2 tablespoons unsalted butter

1 large onion, chopped

1 celery rib, chopped

1 large carrot, peeled and coarsely chopped

4 cups chicken broth

1 teaspoon dried thyme

½ teaspoon crumbled dried sage

⅓ cup half-and-half or light cream

TOPPING

1 recipe Tender Buttermilk Biscuit Crust (page 35)

1   Put 1 cup of the flour in a paper bag or shallow bowl and set it aside. Rinse the chicken pieces, set them aside on a baking sheet lined with paper towels, and blot dry. Salt and pepper the pieces on both sides.

2   Heat the olive oil in a large, heavy, stovetop casserole over medium heat. Add the chicken pieces to the bag, about half at a time—or dredge them in the flour in the bowl—then add them to the casserole without crowding them too much. Brown for 3 minutes on each side, then set aside on a platter. Repeat for the remaining pieces of chicken.

3   Melt the butter in the casserole, and add the onion, celery, and carrot. Cook the vegetables for about 8 minutes, stirring often, then return the chicken to the pan. Add the broth, thyme, sage, and ¼ to ½ teaspoon salt, depending on the saltiness of your broth. Bring to a low boil, then lower the heat and simmer, covered, for 30 minutes. Remove from the heat.

4   Using a slotted spoon, transfer the chicken to a platter. Set the liquid aside for 1 hour to cool. After an hour, use a large spoon to skim off as much of the fat as possible from the top of the liquid. When the chicken has cooled, pick off the meat from the skin and bones, shredding it by hand, and return it to the pot.

5   Preheat the oven to 400°F. Reheat the chicken in the broth over medium heat. In a small bowl, whisk the half-and-half with the remaining ⅓ cup flour until smooth. Stir this thickener into the pot and simmer the chicken mixture over medium heat until full bodied and saucy, 5 to 8 minutes. (You can add another 1 to 1½ tablespoons flour, if necessary. Whisk it into a spoonful of milk first.) Ladle the hot filling into an oiled medium-size baking dish. The filling should come no closer than 1 inch to the top of the dish.

6   Prepare the biscuits as directed, patting or gently rolling them out a little more than ½ inch thick. Cut into rounds, using a 1¾- to 2¼-inch biscuit cutter. Gently place the biscuits on top of the filling, evenly spaced. Put the casserole in the oven and bake until the biscuits are golden brown and the chicken is bubbling, about 25 minutes. Transfer to a rack and cool for 10 to 15 minutes before serving.

Recipe for Success

This is not a dish that I typically make from start to finish in one stretch. In fact, there are two main pause points here that I like to take advantage of. The first is when the broth and chicken cool off; you could refrigerate everything at this point and proceed later that same day or the next. Another is when the now-saucy chicken goes in the casserole that you're going to bake it in. You can cover the casserole and refrigerate it overnight, then place it in a 400°F oven until it's bubbly hot, 35 to 45 minutes. Slide it out, gently deposit the biscuits on top, then bake until done, 25 to 30 minutes more.

Come to think of it, you could also mix up the dry ingredients for the biscuits ahead of time, cut in the butter, then cover and refrigerate overnight. Then all you need to do the next day is add the buttermilk and mix.

The ideal time to eat any biscuit-type dinner pie is 15 to 20 minutes out of the oven. If you wait too long, the biscuits start to absorb a lot of moisture and the filling becomes less saucy. Something to keep in mind.

CHICKEN & RICE CHEESE STRUDEL

This is one of my favorite recipes in this entire collection, a sort of casserole-within-a-pastry. We make a row of chicken and rice down the center of a rectangle of dough, then cut the sides into strips and fold them over the filling, creating a savory strudel that adults and kids alike will devour. Serve with cold applesauce, and something crisp and light on the side, like a chopped salad. **Makes 6 servings**

1 recipe Go-To Pie Dough (page 22), refrigerated

FILLING

2 tablespoons olive oil

½ large onion, chopped

2 garlic cloves, minced

3 to 4 ounces coarsely chopped baby spinach

½ cup chicken broth

2 cups cooked rice

1½ cups chopped cooked chicken

⅓ cup sour cream

1 to 1½ cups grated sharp cheddar, fontina, or Gouda cheese

1 egg yolk beaten with 1 tablespoon milk

Sesame seeds, for sprinkling on top

1   If you haven't already, prepare the pastry and refrigerate it for at least 1½ hours.

2   Heat the olive oil in a large skillet over medium heat. Add the onion and sauté for 7 to 8 minutes. Stir in the garlic and spinach. Sauté briefly, then stir in the chicken broth. Cook briefly to reduce the liquid slightly, then stir in the rice, chicken, ¼ teaspoon salt, and ground black pepper to taste. Continue to cook and stir a minute or two longer, just until warmed. Remove from the heat and stir in the sour cream. Taste, and add more salt if you like. Transfer to a shallow bowl and set aside to cool for 15 minutes. Preheat the oven to 375°F and get out a large baking sheet.

3   After 15 minutes, gently stir the cheese into the rice mixture. Roll the pastry into a 10 x 15-inch rectangle on a large sheet of parchment paper. (If you don't have parchment paper, you can roll and assemble this on a floured work surface, then move it to your baking sheet; or you can roll the dough, transfer it to your baking sheet, and assemble it there.) Mentally divide the dough into three lengthwise sections, then make a neat, mounded row of the filling down the middle section, leaving about 1½ inches of dough uncovered at both ends. Make a couple of notches on each end, creating a little flap of dough that you can fold up over the filling.

4 Now take a paring knife or dough scraper and cut the uncovered portions of dough on the sides into 1½-inch-wide strips, perpendicular to the filling. Starting at one of the ends, fold a strip diagonally over the filling, then fold the strip on the opposite side diagonally over the first one. Brush the end of each strip with a little of the egg wash, then continue folding the strips over the filling, alternating from side to side and brushing with egg wash. When you're done, lift the parchment and strudel onto your baking sheet. Lightly brush the entire surface with egg wash and sprinkle liberally with sesame seeds.

5 Bake the strudel on the center oven rack until the pastry is a rich golden brown, 40 to 45 minutes. Transfer to a rack and cool for at least 15 minutes before serving.

Recipe for Success

One of the keys to success here is making sure that the filling is properly moist, not dry. That's why we add both chicken broth and sour cream to the leftover rice, which tends to dry out as it sits in the fridge. So, just before stirring in the cheese, have a taste of the rice and, if it seems to need a little more broth, go ahead and stir in a few extra tablespoons.

Instead of spinach, you could add chopped broccoli florets to the rice. Add the broccoli when you would have added the spinach, heating until almost tender.

KALE SPANAKOPITA

I love spinach, but substituting kale for the traditional leafy greens in this classic Greek dish is a great way to put a fresh spin on a dinner pie most everyone loves. Our version includes the requisite feta cheese, but it's lightened with some ricotta and sharpened with Parmesan. You can cook up a couple of batches of fresh kale if you like, but this recipe specifies frozen kale to help streamline the prep. In either case, make sure you squeeze most of the liquid out of the kale before mixing it with the cheeses, to avoid a soggy bottom crust. It's fun to see who, if anyone, realizes you've used kale instead of spinach. Have the recipe handy if you bring this to a potluck; you'll get requests for it. **Makes 9 servings**

1½ pounds frozen kale

3 tablespoons unsalted butter

1 large onion, chopped

4 scallions, finely chopped

3 garlic cloves, minced

2 large eggs

¾ cup ricotta cheese

1½ cups crumbled feta cheese

½ cup grated Parmesan cheese

⅓ cup finely chopped fresh
  flat-leaf parsley

2 tablespoons chopped fresh dill

Pinch or two of ground nutmeg

About ¼ cup olive oil

9 sheets phyllo dough, thawed if
  frozen

1 Cook the kale according to the package directions and drain it well in a colander, pressing with a fork to expel excess liquid. When it has cooled enough to handle, squeeze it between your hands to get out even more liquid. However, don't try to get it bone dry; the filling will benefit from a little moisture. Transfer the kale to a platter.

2 Melt the butter in a large skillet over medium heat and stir in the onion and scallions. Cook, stirring often, for 7 to 8 minutes. Stir in the garlic, cook for 30 seconds, then stir in the kale. Heat for 1 minute, stirring, then remove from the heat and set aside.

3 Whisk together the eggs and ricotta cheese in a large bowl to combine evenly. Stir in the feta cheese, Parmesan cheese, parsley, dill, and nutmeg. Add the kale and stir until evenly combined. Salt and pepper the filling to taste, but use a light hand with the salt since the cheeses are already salty.

Don't Fear the Phyllo

With apologies to all the upstanding phyllo workers of America, I somehow always end up with the box that was packaged by the fellow whose wife just told him, that very morning, that he is a world-class loser and she's moving to Maui with her Pilates instructor: My sheets are hopelessly stuck together—stomped on, I imagine—and rare is the occasion when I can peel off a whole sheet without incident. If that sounds familiar, just do the best you can with the sheets, piecing them together if a section turns up missing. The good thing about phyllo is that once your dish is all assembled and baked, no one will ever be able to tell there were issues. The only thing you'll be hearing is the satisfied groans of your tablemates.

4   Preheat the oven to 375°F. Get out a 9-inch square baking dish and oil it well with some of the olive oil. Center one sheet of phyllo over the pan and tuck it down gently into the creases. Brush with olive oil. Center another sheet over the pan, with the length of the sheet running in the opposite direction. Tuck it into the pan and oil that one. Add three more sheets, alternating the direction and oiling each time, for a total of five.

5   Spread the filling evenly in the phyllo-lined baking dish, then fold the overhanging sections of phyllo back over the filling. Layer and oil the remaining four sheets of phyllo on top of the filling, folding it back onto itself to fit in the dish. Using the bristles of your pastry brush or a butter knife, go along the edge and push-tuck the edges down so they're nice and neat.

6   Using a serrated knife, score the phyllo layers—place a ruler on top of the pan, if you like, to guide you—into 9 equal portions. Place on the center oven rack and bake until the top is golden brown and the filling has puffed up a bit, about 40 minutes. Transfer to a rack and cool for at least 30 minutes before serving; the filling will settle as it cools.

Recipe for Success

My local supermarket sells a good house brand of frozen chopped kale. But it does have quite a few stems in it, which I always pick out and discard. My first choice for vegetables is almost always fresh, but there are occasions when I don't mind using a good frozen brand to save a little time.

Whenever I buy fresh herbs, like dill, I make a mental note about what other things I'll use them for, and as soon as possible. I feel so wasteful when fresh herbs linger in my fridge and become unusable because of neglect. With dill, for example, I'll plan to make a salmon quiche (page 128), or I'll add it to a salad dressing or potato salad. Keeping close tabs on leftovers is always good practice and can save you hundreds—even thousands—of dollars a year by avoiding waste.

FRESH TOMATO & HAM COBBLER

This cobbler was inspired by a James Beard tomato pie recipe that, I believe, first appeared in *James Beard's American Cookery* (1972). The Beard version uses tomatoes and corn instead of the ham, and mayo instead of the ranch dressing. But they do have a biscuit-style crust in common, mine being a cornmeal biscuit. The thicker biscuit crust is the perfect sponge for the savory juices. (I use the same basic crust for Clyde's Chili Biscuit Cobbler on page 213 and the Baked Reuben Sandwich on page 54.) If you like a grilled cheese and tomato sandwich, you're going to love this. **Makes 8 servings**

1 recipe Cornmeal Biscuit Crust (page 34), divided as instructed in step 1 and refrigerated

FILLING

3 medium-large ripe tomatoes

3 tablespoons dry Italian-style bread crumbs

2 to 3 tablespoons minced fresh Italian herbs, such as basil, rosemary, oregano, and thyme, in whatever combination you like best

3 garlic cloves, minced

⅔ cup ranch dressing

1½ cups grated sharp cheddar cheese

½ cup diced ham

1 If you haven't already, prepare the biscuit dough for the crust. Turn the dough out onto a floured work surface and divide it in half, making one half a little larger than the other. (The larger half is for the bottom crust.) Using floured hands, gently knead each portion several times. Flour the dough and place each portion on individual sheets of plastic wrap. Flatten into ¾-inch-thick disks. Wrap and refrigerate for 45 minutes to 1 hour. While the dough chills, butter a 9½-inch deep-dish pie pan. Set aside.

2 Unwrap the larger portion of dough and give it a good dusting of flour on each side (leave the smaller one in the refrigerator). Place the dough between two sheets of plastic wrap and roll it into a circle 12½ inches in diameter. Remove the top plastic and invert the biscuit dough over the pie pan. Peel off the plastic and gently nudge the dough into the pan. Refrigerate for 15 minutes. Adjust the oven rack so it is one position above the bottom shelf. Preheat the oven to 375°F.

3 Core and halve the tomatoes, squeezing out much—but not all—of the seeds; you want some of the juice in the pie. Thinly slice the tomatoes and set them aside on a plate. Mix the bread crumbs, herbs, and garlic in a small bowl. Set aside.

4 To layer the pie, start by sprinkling one-quarter of the crumbs in the bottom of the shell. Layer one-third of the tomatoes in the shell; salt and pepper them to taste. Dollop with one-third of the ranch dressing, then cover with one-third of the cheese and one-third of the ham. Top with another one-quarter of the crumb mixture. Make two more layers just like the first one—tomatoes, salt and pepper, dressing, cheese, ham, and crumbs.

5   Unwrap the other portion of dough, flour it, and roll into a circle 10 to 10½ inches in diameter. Using a wet fingertip, moisten the edge of the pie shell, then drape the rolled dough over the top. Press the edges together to seal. Using a serrated knife, make a couple of shallow slits in the top dough for steam vents.

6   Bake for about 45 minutes. When done, the crust should look good and brown. If you don't actually see juices bubbling up through the slits, you will likely hear them. If you're in doubt, cover the top with foil—so the top doesn't get too dark—and continue to bake for another 5 to 7 minutes. Transfer to a rack and cool for 15 to 20 minutes before serving.

Recipe for Success

If it seems a little tedious or fussy to refrigerate this biscuit dough, it's worth it. The chilling makes it much easier to handle and you'll avoid a lot of sticking grief if you chill.

It's optional, but you can brush a little heavy cream on top of the dough before you bake this. It'll add some shine and a bit of crunch to the topping.

CLYDE'S CHILI BISCUIT COBBLER

Clyde is my father-in-law, an inventive cook who grew into his craft hunting and fishing his way through a West Virginia childhood, spending 22 years in the Marine Corps, and then a decade or so shrimping and cooking up the best seafood the South Carolina Lowcountry has to offer. The inspiration for this dish is all Clyde's, though I have—the way most cooks do—fiddled and tweaked with it to add my personal stamp. The concept, great chili with a biscuit topping, is simple, and the flavor is fabulous. It's the perfect cold weather dish. See the Recipe for Success on page 214 for the condiment pep talk; Clyde says it's required reading. **Makes 6 to 8 servings**

2 tablespoons vegetable oil

1 large onion, finely chopped

1 large green bell pepper, seeded and finely chopped

1½ pounds ground chuck

3 garlic cloves, minced

2 tablespoons chili powder

1½ teaspoons ground cumin

1 teaspoon smoked paprika

1 (28-ounce) can diced tomatoes, with their juice

2 (15-ounce) cans pinto beans, rinsed and drained

1½ cups beef broth, or more if needed

1 cup tomato sauce

3 tablespoons Heinz chili sauce

2 tablespoons tomato paste, or more to taste

1 tablespoon barbecue sauce

1 tablespoon light brown sugar

TOPPING

1 recipe Cornmeal Biscuit Crust (page 34)

1   Heat the oil in a large stovetop casserole or Dutch oven over medium heat. Add the onion and green pepper and sauté for 6 to 7 minutes. Stir in the ground chuck. Brown the meat thoroughly, breaking it up with a wooden spoon as it cooks. When the meat has browned, remove the pot from the heat, tilt it, and spoon off and discard all but 2 to 3 tablespoons of the fat.

2   Put the pot back on the heat and stir in the garlic, chili powder, cumin, and paprika. Cook for 1 minute, stirring. Stir in the rest of the chili ingredients, along with ½ teaspoon salt and ground black pepper to taste.

3   Bring the mixture to a simmer and cook, stirring occasionally, for 15 to 20 minutes. The chili should stay nice and saucy because the biscuits will need the liquid as they cook. If it starts to get too thick, add up to ½ cup additional broth. And if it needs a little more body, add another tablespoon of tomato paste. Season to taste with more salt and pepper if needed.

4   If the pot you've been cooking in doesn't dwarf the amount of chili—in which case, the top crust would not get properly browned—you can also just leave the chili in the pot and finish baking the cobbler right in it. Otherwise, when the chili is done simmering, transfer it to a smaller casserole dish that you have lightly oiled. Preheat the oven to 400°F.

Continued

5 Prepare the dough as instructed; however, since you will not be rolling it out like a pie crust, it's not crucial that you chill the dry mixture. On a floured work surface, pat or roll the dough about ½ inch thick. Using a 1½- to 2-inch round biscuit cutter, cut the dough and place the circles, evenly spaced, on top of the chili. Be sure to gather the scraps and cut them, too. Bake until the biscuits are cooked through and golden brown, 15 to 20 minutes. Cool briefly, then serve.

Recipe for Success

This recipe does make quite a bit of chili, more than you may need for your meal. If that's the case, I suggest refrigerating or freezing some of it for later. Transfer the amount of chili you do want to use to a medium-size casserole, filling it about two-thirds full. Then roll (or pat) your dough, cut your biscuits, and place them on top. (The smaller your casserole, the thicker your biscuits will need to be.) This won't leave you with any biscuit topping for the portion you saved, but that's okay; the chili is great on its own.

Clyde never serves this dish without an entire smorgasbord of garnishes, each in its own little bowl: sour cream, grated cheddar or Monterey Jack cheese, shredded iceberg lettuce, sliced olives, pickled jalapeño pepper slices, salsa, and more. It's just not the same without.

MEATLOAF WELLINGTON

Here's beef Wellington's casual cousin, a dish I've also heard referred to as "poor man's beef Wellington." In place of the pricey and more formal beef tenderloin, we wrap our pastry around a big log of perfectly seasoned beef and sausage meatloaf. It makes for a hip food-fashion statement, like one of those country singers who shows up on awards night in a tuxedo jacket and blue jeans. If you want to sauce this with a little something, I like to blend equal parts mustardy barbecue sauce and Heinz chili sauce and warm the mixture in the microwave or a saucepan. Mashed potatoes or potatoes au gratin on the side, please. **Makes 6 to 8 servings**

1 recipe Go-To Pie Dough (page 22), prepared as instructed in step 1 and refrigerated

FILLING

2 tablespoons olive oil

½ cup finely chopped onion

½ cup finely chopped carrot

¼ cup finely chopped green bell pepper

3 garlic cloves, minced

1 large egg

3 tablespoons whole milk

2 tablespoons Heinz chili sauce

1 teaspoon Dijon mustard

1 teaspoon Worcestershire sauce

Several shakes of Tabasco or other hot sauce

1 pound lean ground beef

8 ounces hot or mild Italian sausage meat, out of the casing

⅓ cup dry Italian-style bread crumbs

1 teaspoon dried thyme

1. Prepare the pastry, but instead of shaping it into a disk, shape it into a square about ¾ inch thick. Cover with plastic wrap and refrigerate for 1½ to 2 hours.

2. Heat the oil in a medium-size skillet over medium heat. Add the onion, carrot, and bell pepper. Sauté until the onion is translucent, 7 to 8 minutes. Stir in the garlic and cook for another minute. Remove from the heat and set aside.

3. In a medium bowl, whisk the egg, milk, chili sauce, mustard, Worcestershire sauce, and Tabasco. Set aside.

4. Combine the beef and sausage in a large mixing bowl, breaking up the meat somewhat with your hands. Add the bread crumbs, thyme, ¾ teaspoon salt, and ¼ teaspoon ground black pepper. Mix by hand for another few seconds to spread everything around. Add the beaten egg mixture. Mix well by hand until evenly combined.

5. Mound the meatloaf on a large piece of parchment paper or wax paper and shape it into a fat 8½-inch-long log. Fold the paper over the meat, put tension on the paper, and sort of roll the meat in the wrap so it takes on a well-rounded shape. Keep the roll as close to 8½ inches long as possible. Wrap the meatloaf up in the paper, seal the ends, and place on a small baking sheet. Refrigerate for 1 hour.

Continued

6   When you're ready to bake, preheat the oven to 350°F. Get out a 5 x 9-inch loaf pan and butter it lightly. Line the long sides and bottom with a single sheet of parchment paper 15 to 16 inches long; you want enough of an overhang to grab when you lift out the meatloaf later.

7   Roll the pastry into a 12-inch square on a lightly floured sheet of wax paper or parchment paper. Remove the meatloaf from the wrapping and place it in the center, as if you were getting ready to wrap a present. Fold one of the sides of the pastry up over the length of the meat, snugly, and moisten the exposed edge with a wet fingertip. Fold up the other long side, overlapping the first one. Press gently together. Fold up the ends of the pastry—again, sort of like wrapping a present—and then place the loaf in the loaf pan, seam side down. Using a serrated knife, make a 2-inch-long slit, lengthwise, in the center of the top of the pastry.

8   Bake the loaf until the juices run clear—you'll see them come out the top slit—and an instant-read thermometer inserted into the center of the loaf registers 160°F, about 1 hour and 15 minutes. Transfer the loaf pan to a cooling rack for 10 to 15 minutes and then, lifting by the overhanging parchment, remove the loaf from the pan and place it on a platter. Cool a bit longer before slicing and serving.

Recipe for Success

When you fold the pastry over the meat, you don't have to pinch it together. The seams are going to end up either under the loaf or hidden at the ends, and the pressure from the expanding loaf will seal them nicely.

I think any meatloaf tastes best when it has had plenty of time to cool, preferably to lukewarm, and the juices have reabsorbed into the loaf. Keep that in mind if you're serving this for a gathering: You can have it out of the oven well before people arrive.

MEASUREMENT EQUIVALENTS

Please note that all conversions are approximate.

LIQUID CONVERSIONS

U.S.	Metric
1 tsp	5 ml
1 tbs	15 ml
2 tbs	30 ml
3 tbs	45 ml
¼ cup	60 ml
⅓ cup	75 ml
⅓ cup + 1 tbs	90 ml
⅓ cup + 2 tbs	100 ml
½ cup	120 ml
⅔ cup	150 ml
¾ cup	180 ml
¾ cup + 2 tbs	200 ml
1 cup	240 ml
1 cup + 2 tbs	275 ml
1¼ cups	300 ml
1⅓ cups	325 ml
1½ cups	350 ml
1⅔ cups	375 ml
1¾ cups	400 ml
1¾ cups + 2 tbs	450 ml
2 cups (1 pint)	475 ml
2½ cups	600 ml
3 cups	720 ml
4 cups (1 quart)	945 ml
	(1,000 ml is 1 liter)

WEIGHT CONVERSIONS

U.S./U.K.	Metric
½ oz	14 g
1 oz	28 g
1½ oz	43 g
2 oz	57 g
2½ oz	71 g
3 oz	85 g
3½ oz	100 g
4 oz	113 g
5 oz	142 g
6 oz	170 g
7 oz	200 g
8 oz	227 g
9 oz	255 g
10 oz	284 g
11 oz	312 g
12 oz	340 g
13 oz	368 g
14 oz	400 g
15 oz	425 g
1 lb	454 g

OVEN TEMPERATURE CONVERSIONS

°F	Gas Mark	°C
250	½	120
275	1	140
300	2	150
325	3	165
350	4	180
375	5	190
400	6	200
425	7	220
450	8	230
475	9	240
500	10	260
550	Broil	290

INDEX

ACKNOWLEDGMENTS

As you can imagine, after more than three decades writing cookbooks and magazine articles, and—more recently—running a website, a fellow can rack up quite a few folks he is indebted to, for one reason or another. Here are some good folks in my life who deserve a word of thanks.

Thanks to the entire crew at The Harvard Common Press—Bruce, Dan, Virginia, Emily, Adam, Pat, and Karen—as well as Jeff McLaughlin, Ashley Prine, and Katherine Furman who recognized the need for a thorough treatment of savory dinner pies, then did such a crack job of launching it into print.

My gratitude goes to Melissa DiPalma, whose lovely photographs grace the pages of this book and make me proud to be the author.

To the dozens of magazine and book editors I've worked with over the years who've encouraged, cajoled, and occasionally browbeaten me to become a better writer, thanks for your counsel and kind words.

My heartfelt gratitude goes to Mom and Dad, for laying the foundation, and to my sibs—Joe, Barb, Tom, Will, Joanne, and Mary—for your blessings.

Thanks to my children—Ben, Tess, Ali, and Sam—whose keen palates and candid feedback *(Cripes, Pop! What IS this stuff?)* helped me grow a Teflon skin when I was starting out in my food career.

To my sweet and beautiful wife, Bev—who prays daily that I will someday write a book about salads, slimming smoothies, or, indeed, virtually anything without a pastry—thank you for your forbearance, love, and loyalty.

Finally, thanks to the several thousand fellow pie makers who have joined me at ThePieAcademy.com to read my articles, find recipes, and learn more about pie making, savory and sweet. It's a blessing to have this platform so I can share my work and passion for pie with you.

ABOUT THE AUTHOR

KEN HAEDRICH is one of America's most respected food writers and a recognized authority on baking, particularly when it comes to pie. He is the "dean" of the popular website ThePieAcademy.com and the author of the best-selling book *Pie Academy* and more than a dozen other cookbooks, including *The Harvest Baker* and *Maple Syrup Cookbook*. Ken is a recipient of the Julia Child Cookbook Award and has been a regular contributor to *Bon Appetit, Better Homes and Gardens, Eating Well* and many other publications. A native of New Jersey and a former Navy Seabee, he and his wife, Bev, make their home in Wilmington, North Carolina.